CHARTING YOUR LEGACY

Designed by Dwayne Bassett of Sprocket Creative
Edited by Steve Gardner and Larry Libby

ISBN 978-1-7348223-6-6

CONTENTS

1

STARTING WELL

For most people, making financial decisions can be compared to driving a car. Their cash and credit limitations serve as clearly defined boundaries. The budget and checkbook balance are like traffic lights for spending – red for stop, green for go, and yellow for caution.

However, for those with significant resources, the boundaries are not so clearly defined. Making financial decisions for these people might be better likened to navigating a ship on the open seas in the 1800s. In those days, there were no GPS systems to follow, directional markers to show you the right way to go, or signs to warn of dangers ahead. The captain had to learn how to navigate using a compass, a sextant, and a timepiece. A telescope would help him see lighthouses warning of danger.

With fewer financial limitations to serve as boundaries, those who have wealth face unusual challenges and opportunities. Fortunately, the Bible provides us with specific instructions, principles, and even warnings to help those entrusted with much as they navigate an ocean of seemingly unlimited choices.

It's important to understand that the biblical truths and cautions addressed to the affluent are intended for your good. God loves you with an unfathomable love. John 15:9 says, *"as the Father has loved me, so have I loved you."* Imagine the depth of love God the Father has for God the Son. In the same way, He loves you! And just as a loving earthly father desires a close relationship with his children, so our heavenly Father hungers for such a relationship with each of us. God knows very well that wealth can present a potential barrier to this intimate relationship with Him.

It is important to realize every time God says, 'You shall not,' He is simply saying, 'Don't hurt yourself,' and when He says, 'You shall,' He means 'help yourself to happiness.' God only wants for us what we would want for ourselves if we were smart enough to want it." – Adrian Rogers

GOD'S ECONOMY

God's economy and the way most people view money are in sharp contrast. This should not surprise us. Isaiah 55:8-9 reads, *"For my thoughts are not your thoughts, neither are your ways my ways,' declares the Lord. 'For as the heavens are higher than the earth, so are my ways higher than your ways, and my thoughts than your thoughts'"* (ESV). God's ways are not only different, they are so much better than our practices! The most significant difference is that in God's economy, the living Lord plays the dominant role. He is central. As elementary as it appears, this distinction has profound implications.

Because God has chosen to be invisible and to operate in the unseen supernatural realm, most people view financial decisions based on the Bible as an illogical leap of faith.

You might be surprised to learn just how much the Bible says about money. More than 2,350 verses relate to handling money and possessions, including fifteen percent of everything Jesus said! There are two primary reasons the Lord said so much about this.

How we handle our money influences our fellowship with the Lord.

This is huge. Jesus equates how we handle our money with the quality of our spiritual lives. In Luke 16:11, He says, *"If then you have not been faithful in the use of worldly wealth, who will entrust the true riches to you?"* If we handle our money properly according to the principles of Scripture, we will grow closer to Christ.

We see this clearly illustrated in the parable of the talents. The master commends the servant who had managed money faithfully: *"Well done, good and faithful servant. You were faithful with a few things, I will put you in charge of many things; **enter into the joy of your master**"* (Matthew 25:21, emphasis added). As we handle money God's way, we have the opportunity to enter into the joy of a more intimate relationship with our Lord.

Someone once told me that the Lord will sometimes allow a person to teach a particular subject because the teacher so desperately needs the content! That was certainly true for me. I've never met anyone who had more wrong attitudes toward money or who handled it in a way more contrary to the principles of Scripture than I did. But when I learned and began to apply these timeless biblical truths, I experienced a dramatic improvement in my fellowship with the Lord. Each of these principles is intended to draw us closer to Christ.

Possessions compete with the Lord for mastery of our lives.

Imagine for a moment that you have never read the Bible, and you are asked to fill in this blank space: "You cannot serve God and _____." What word would you choose? Why?

It surprises many to learn that money is a primary competitor with Christ for the lordship of our lives. In fact, Jesus Himself tells us we must choose to serve only one of these two masters. *"No servant can serve two masters, for either he will hate the one and love the other, or he will be devoted to one and despise the other. You cannot serve God and Money"* (Luke 16:13).

In the next verses, we are warned that many will reject this message. *"The Pharisees* [religious leaders]*, who were lovers of money, heard all these things, and they ridiculed him* [Jesus]*. And he said to them, 'You are those who justify yourselves before men, but God knows your hearts. For what is exalted among men is an abomination in the sight of God"* (Luke 16:14-15).

God realizes that it is impossible for us to serve money – even in a small way – and still serve Him. When the Crusades were being fought during the twelfth century, the Crusaders purchased the services of mercenaries to fight on their behalf. Because it was a religious war, the Crusaders insisted that the mercenaries be baptized before fighting. As they were being baptized, the mercenaries would take their swords and hold them out of the water to symbolize that Jesus Christ was not in control of their swords. They wanted to retain the freedom to use their swords in any way they wished.

Though many people today may not be as blatant about it as were the mercenaries, they often handle their money in a similar fashion. Some Christians hold a wallet, purse, or stock portfolio "out of the water." In effect, these people are saying, "God, You may be the Lord of my entire life, except in the area of money – I am perfectly capable of handling that myself." Martin Luther recognized this struggle when he said, "There are three conversions: the conversion of the heart, of the mind and of the pocketbook."

The Lord talked so much about money because he knew that much of our lives would revolve around its use. During your normal week, how much time do you spend earning money in your job, making decisions on how to spend money, thinking about where to invest money, or praying about your giving? Fortunately, God has adequately prepared us by giving us the Bible as His blueprint for living.

FINISHING WELL IS RARE

When people used to ask evangelist Billy Graham how they could pray for him, he invariably responded, "Pray that I finish my life well and don't dishonor the Lord." He recognized how rare it is for people to remain faithful to the Lord and engaged in fulfilling their calling to the end.

According to Dr. Howard Hendricks, of the 2,930 individuals mentioned in the Bible, we know significant details about only 100 of them. Of those 100, only about one-third finished well. Of the two-thirds that did not finish well, most failed in the second half of their lives. Finishing well for those who are wealthy is especially challenging because of the options money can buy. Many of these can distract us from serving the Lord.

Few people have started well with more promise than Solomon. Consider this:

- He was loved by God before he was born. *"The Lord loved* [Solomon]; *and because the Lord loved him, he sent word through Nathan the prophet to name him Jedidiah* [which means loved by the Lord] (2 Samuel 12:24-25, NIV).

- He was successor to the throne of his father, King David. David was described as a man *"after God's own heart"* (1 Samuel 13:14) and authored most of the book of Psalms.

- He was given extraordinary wisdom. *"The Lord appeared to Solomon during the night in a dream, and God said, 'Ask for whatever you want me to give you'"* (1 Kings 3:5, NIV). Solomon asked for wisdom to lead God's people. God was pleased with his request and said, *"I will give you a wise and discerning heart, so that there will never have been anyone like you, nor will there ever be"* (1 Kings 3:12-13, NIV). Solomon wrote most of the book of Proverbs.

Later Solomon tragically descended into a life of disobedience and refusal to follow the Lord. Deuteronomy 17 lists three things the kings of Israel were prohibited from doing. Compare them with Solomon's actions.

- *"The king must not acquire great numbers of horses for himself or make the people return to Egypt to get more of them"* (Deuteronomy 17:16, NIV).

"Solomon had 40,000 stalls of horses for his chariots, and 12,000 horsemen" (1 Kings 4:26). *"Solomon's horses were imported from Egypt . . ."* (1 Kings 10:28, NIV).

- *"He must not take many wives, or his heart will be led astray"* (Deuteronomy 17:17, NIV).

*"King Solomon, however, loved many foreign women . . . They were from nations about which the Lord had told the Israelites, 'You must not intermarry with them, because they will surely turn your hearts after their gods.' Nevertheless, Solomon held fast to them in love. He had seven hundred wives of royal birth and three hundred concubines, and **his wives led him astray**"* (1 Kings 11:1-3, NIV, emphasis added).

- *"He must not accumulate large amounts of silver and gold"* (Deuteronomy 17:17, NIV).

"I [Solomon] *amassed silver and gold for myself, and the treasure of kings and provinces"* (Ecclesiastes 2:8, NIV).

Solomon's refusal to obey and worship the true God led to idolatry. The consequences were disastrous for Solomon, his family, and for the entire nation of Israel. Starting well does not guarantee that a person will finish well, regardless of possessing great wisdom, wealth, fame, authority, or godly ancestors.

An effective strategy when planning to accomplish a major task is to begin with the end in mind. The goal of this book is that you would commit to *finish well* in ways that please the Lord. Each chapter is designed to help you achieve that objective in a different area of your life.

⬤ PERSONAL REFLECTIONS

View the Story.

View the Alan and Katherine Barnhart video – God Owns Our Business (17:07) at ChartingYourLegacy.org, or by using this QR code.

- What were the most encouraging and challenging parts of the Barnhart story?

- Describe anything from their video that you will attempt to apply.

GOD'S PART

When it comes to the responsibility of handling money, the Bible shows us a clear division.

God has a part, and we have a part.

It really is that simple. In other words, the Lord has retained certain responsibilities while delegating others to us. Most of the frustration we experience in handling money grows out of our difficulty in determining which responsibilities are ours and which are His.

When the captain of that 1800s sailing vessel I mentioned found himself in the open sea with no view of land, he depended on determining due north to keep his bearing and reach his destination. At night, he would locate the North Star and use it to maintain his course. He zeroed in on that North Star as if his life, his ship and all the souls on board depended on it, because they did.

For the wealthy faced with the challenges of handling money and assets biblically in an "ocean of choices without boundaries," their North Star is understanding God's Part. If you miss this North Star, then every other financial decision you make is correspondingly skewed.

In the Bible, God calls Himself by more than 250 names. The name that best describes God's part in the area of money is *Lord*.

For example, after losing his ten children and all his wealth – in a single day! – Job continued to worship God, saying, *"The LORD gave and the LORD has taken away. Blessed be the name of the LORD"* (Job 1:21). Even in his grief, he understood God's role as Lord of his possessions.

Moses walked away from the treasures of Egypt, choosing instead to suffer with God's people, because he accepted God's role as Lord of all. There are several facets to God's role.

Ownership

The Lord is the Creator of everything. *"For by Him* [Jesus Christ] *all things were created, both in the heavens and on earth, visible and invisible . . . all things have been created through Him and for Him. . . . and in Him all things hold together"* (Colossians 1:16-17). The Lord not only created everything, but also holds everything together. And by the way, He has never transferred the ownership of His creation to people.

There is nothing that twists the soul more than to think wrongly about God." – A.W. Tozer

Whether you realize it or not, whether you acknowledge it or not, the Lord owns all your possessions. *"The earth is the LORD's and **everything** in it, the world and all who live in it"* (Psalm 24:1, NIV, emphasis added). *"Everything in the heavens and earth is yours, O Lord . . ."* (1 Chronicles 29:11, TLB). How much do you own? NOTHING! ZERO!

Scripture even reveals specific items He owns.

- God owns all the land. *"The land, moreover, shall not be sold permanently, for the land is Mine; for you are but aliens and sojourners with Me"* (Leviticus 25:23).

- God owns all the silver and gold. *"The silver is Mine, and the gold is Mine," declares the Lord of hosts* (Haggai 2:8).

- God owns all the animals. *"For every beast of the forest is Mine, the cattle on a thousand hills. . . . everything that moves in the field is Mine. If I were hungry I would not tell you, for the world is Mine, and all it contains"* (Psalm 50:12).

If we truly want to be genuine followers of Christ, we must transfer ownership of our possessions to the Lord. *"So then, none of you can be My disciple who does not give up **all** his own possessions"* (Luke 14:33, emphasis added). We must give up all claim to the ownership of all we have. Sometimes the Lord will test us by asking that we be willing to relinquish the very thing most precious to us.

The most vivid example of this in the Bible is when the Lord asked Abraham to *"Take now your son, your only son, whom you love, Isaac . . . and offer him there as a burnt offering"* (Genesis 22:2). When Abraham obeyed, demonstrating his willingness to give up his dear son, God responded, *"Do not stretch out your hand against the lad . . . for now I know that you fear God, since you have not withheld your son, your only son, from Me"* (Genesis 22:12).

When we acknowledge God's ownership, every spending decision becomes a spiritual decision. Instead of asking, "Lord, what do You want me to do with **my** money?" the question becomes, "Lord, what do You want me to do with **Your** money?" When we have this perspective and handle His money according to His wishes, spending and investing decisions are equally as spiritual as giving decisions.

As we will see throughout this book, recognizing God's ownership is key to allowing Jesus Christ to become the Lord of our money and possessions.

Is it easy? Of course not. Nobody said it would be! Consistently recognizing God's ownership is difficult. It's way too easy to fall into the trap of making an intellectual assent to God's ownership without letting that truth filter down into the nitty-gritty of daily life – especially because our culture constantly trumpets an opposing view. Everything around us – the media, even the law – says that what you possess, you and you alone own. Genuinely acknowledging God's ownership requires nothing less than a total change of perception.

To help you recognize God's ownership, meditate on this passage for the next thirty days when you first awake and just before going to sleep.

> *"Everything in the heavens and earth is yours, O Lord, and this is your kingdom. We adore you as being in control of everything. Riches and honor come from you alone, and you are the ruler of all mankind; your hand controls power and might, and it is at your discretion that men are made great and given strength"* (1 Chronicles 29:11-12, TLB).

Success and Wealth

How many times have we heard stories of individuals pulling themselves up by their bootstraps and becoming proud, self-made men or women of achievement? It's certainly true that the creation of wealth usually requires great personal effort, but Scripture reveals that God plays the most important role. Consider this:

God gives us the ability to make wealth. *"He gave you manna to eat in the desert, something your fathers had never known, to humble and to test you, so that in the end it might go well with you. Otherwise, you may say in your heart, 'My power and the strength of my hand made me this wealth.'* **But remember the LORD your God, for it is he who gives you the ability to produce wealth"** (Deuteronomy 8:16-18, NIV, emphasis added).

God controls our promotion. Psalm 75:6-7 reads, *"For promotion and power come from nowhere on earth, but only from God"* (TLB). As much as it may surprise people, their boss is not the one who controls whether they will be promoted. It is the Lord alone who promotes.

God gives us our success. The life of Joseph is a perfect example of God working behind the scene to accomplish His purpose by elevating a person. *"The LORD was with Joseph, so he became a successful man. . . . his master saw that the LORD was with him and how the Lord caused all that he did to prosper in his hand"* (Genesis 39:2-3).

God teaches us to profit. *"Thus says the* LORD, *your Redeemer, the Holy One of Israel, 'I am the Lord your God, who teaches you to profit, who leads you in the way you should go'"* (Isaiah 48:17).

God is responsible for our accomplishments. *". . . all that we have accomplished you* [Lord] *have done for us"* (Isaiah 26:12, NIV).

God gives us our skills. Exodus 36:1 illustrates this truth: *"And every skillful person in whom the* LORD *has put skill and understanding to know how to perform all the work."* This verse applies to all of us. God has given each of us unique skills. People have widely varied abilities, manual skills, intellectual capacities, and sometimes hidden reservoirs of giftedness. It's not a matter of one person being better than another; it is simply a matter of having received different abilities. The true story of God's role in creating an individual's wealth stands in stark contrast to the assumptions of our culture. Most people believe that they alone are responsible for their job skills, success, promotions, and wealth creation.

A major contributor to wrong attitudes about money is not understanding God's role. For a few minutes, reflect on God's role. He is the owner of everything you have ever had or ever will have. He gives you your skills, controls success and promotion, opens doors of opportunity for you, and provides you with necessary creativity and abilities.

In Psalm 139:3-5 David realized this truth when he wrote: *"You* [Lord] *chart the path ahead of me and tell me where to stop and rest. Every moment you know where I am. You know what I am going to say before I even say it. You both precede and follow me and place your hand of blessing on my head."* (TLB)

How should this perspective impact your thinking?

God entrusts assets for a purpose.

The Lord chooses different ways of entrusting people with significant assets: some inherit, others marry into a wealthy family, and still others develop a practice or a business or manage investments well. Regardless of *how* you have become wealthy, God has allowed this for a special purpose.

God has chosen to entrust you with much. Simply acknowledging this, you shouldn't feel guilty or carry around a sense of condemnation for what you have been provided. God has given each person a particular calling in order to accomplish His plan for history. Acts 13:36 confirms this, *"For David, after he had served the purpose of God in his own generation, fell asleep, and was laid among his fathers."* Handling your assets God's way is a major part of His purpose for you. This *Charting Your Legacy* book is designed to help you discover or better understand God's purpose for you.

It's not wrong to be rich; it's wrong to be rich and not ask why we've been entrusted with much." – Unknown

GETTING TO KNOW GOD

God, as He is revealed in the Bible, differs greatly from the way people commonly imagine Him. Our tendency is to shrink God down and fit Him into a mold with human abilities and limitations. We have a hard time recognizing God's Part because we fail to understand the greatness of God, *"who stretched out the heavens and laid the foundations of the earth"* (Isaiah 51:13). How do we capture the true perspective of God? Primarily by learning what the Bible tells us about Him.

I love how the patriarch Job described Him: *"God stretches out heaven over empty space and hangs the earth upon nothing. He wraps the rain in his thick clouds and the clouds, are not split by the weight. He shrouds his throne with his clouds. He sets a boundary for the ocean, yes, and a boundary for the day and for the night. The pillars of heaven tremble at his rebuke. . . These are some of the minor things he does, merely a whisper of his power. Who then can withstand his thunder?"* (Job 26:7-11, 14, TLB)

Here are a few more samples:

He is Lord of the universe.

Carefully review some of His names and attributes:

Creator	Omniscient
Almighty	Lord of lords
Eternal	King of kings
Omnipresent	Savior

The Lord's power and ability are incomprehensible. Astronomers estimate that there are more than 100 billion galaxies in the universe, each containing billions of stars. The distance from one end of a galaxy to the other is often measured in millions of light years. Though our sun is a relatively small star, it could contain over one million earths, and it sustains temperatures of 20 million degrees at its center. The enormity of the universe is mind boggling. *"Lift up your eyes on high and see who has created these stars, the One who leads forth their host by number, He calls them all by name; because of the greatness of His might and the strength of His power not one of them is missing"* (Isaiah 40:26). How can we even read this verse without mouthing a silent "Wow!"

He is Lord of the nations.

Examine the Lord's role and position relative to nations and people. Isaiah 40:21-24 tells us, *"Do you not know? Have you not heard? . . . It is He who sits above the circle of the earth, and its inhabitants are like grasshoppers . . . He it is who reduces rulers to nothing, who makes the judges of the earth meaningless. Scarcely have they been planted, scarcely have they been sown, scarcely has their stock taken root in the earth, but He merely blows on them, and they wither."*

From Isaiah 40:15,17 we read, *"Behold, the nations are like a drop from a bucket, and are regarded as a speck of dust on the scales . . . all the nations are as nothing before Him, they are regarded by Him as less than nothing and meaningless."*

He is Lord of each individual.

God is not some aloof, disinterested, impersonal "force." On the contrary, He is intimately involved with each of us as individuals. Psalm 139:3-4, 16 reveals, *"You are familiar with all my ways. Before a word is on my tongue you know it completely, O Lord. . . . All the days ordained for me were written in your book before one of them came to be"* (NIV). The Lord is so involved in our lives that He reassures us, *"The very hairs of your head are all numbered"* (Matthew 10:30). Our heavenly Father is the One who knows us the best and loves us the most.

God hung the stars in space, fashioned the earth's towering mountains and mighty oceans, and determined the destiny of nations. Jeremiah observed correctly: *"Nothing is too difficult for You"* (Jeremiah 32:17). Yet this is the same God who knows when a sparrow falls to the ground. He is the Lord of the vast universe and yet chooses to involve Himself in the smallest details of your life. *Nothing in this book is more important than catching the vision of who God is and what His part is in our life and finances.*

When I first studied God's Part, there was nothing that particularly surprised me. I knew all these truths – vaguely. My problem is that I don't always live as if they are actually true. In contemporary culture, God is thought to play no part in financial matters, and we have in some measure been influenced by this view.

Another reason for this difficulty is that God has chosen to be invisible. As Paul declared, He is *"the King eternal, immortal, invisible, the only God"* (1 Timothy 1:17, NIV).

Anything that is "out of sight," however, tends to become "out of mind." And even though I don't intend it, I get out of the habit of recognizing consistently that He is the Owner.

After learning God's Part, some quickly jump to the conclusion that little responsibility remains for us. But this is far from being true! As we study Our Part, we will discover the Lord has entrusted us with great responsibility.

✎ PERSONAL REFLECTIONS

View the Louie Giglio video – Our God is Indescribable (7:55) at ChartingYourLegacy.org, or by using this QR code.

- Reflect on God's role in any success you have experienced and in the creation of your wealth. How does this influence your perspective?

3

OUR PART

Henry Parsons Crowell was born into a wealthy family, and as a young man received a large inheritance when his father died. He could have quit work that very day, adopting a life of leisure for the rest of his days. But that's not the option he chose. Instead, young Crowell decided to work hard, committing to give ten percent of his income to the Lord's work.

Crowell founded the Quaker Oats Company, and he proved to be an amazingly creative marketing genius. At that time oats were sold in large barrels, often rotting before being consumed. Crowell introduced the smaller round packaging we are familiar with to this day, and determined to use only the highest quality oats. His company became remarkably successful and literally changed the way Americans ate breakfast.

In 1898, Crowell's perspective on money and business was radically transformed by participating in a Bible study on money and possessions. *Not only are we to honor Christ in our company*, he thought to himself, *but everything we have belongs to God – even the business.*

Recognizing this changed everything! He felt as if he had been elevated from the role of just operating *his* business and handling *his* money, to the most important position possible – a person entrusted with managing *God's* business and resources. For more than 40 years, he gave away over half of his earnings.

Henry Parsons Crowell had embraced the most significant truths for the follower of Christ in handling money – Ownership and Stewardship.[1]

What is a steward?

The word that best describes Our Part is *steward.* Today we would probably use the word "manager." In the Bible, the position of steward is one of great responsibility. He is the supreme authority under the master and has full responsibility for all the master's possessions entrusted to him.

It's also helpful to think of being the trustee of a trust. The trustee has a legal fiduciary responsibility to handle the assets of the trust according to the terms and provisions of the trust. The trustee does not have unbridled freedom to manage the assets any way he or she chooses. In a similar way, God has placed certain assets into our care, and He has conveyed His wishes to us in a trust document, the Bible.

Our responsibility is to be faithful. *"It is required of stewards that one be found faithful"* (1 Corinthians 4:2, NKJV). Before we can be faithful, however, we need to take stock of our responsibilities. What does God desire and expect from us? Just as the trustee studies the trust document to learn how to properly manage the trust assets, we need to examine the Creator's handbook – the Bible – to determine how He wants us to handle His possessions. Those who are wealthy bear a particularly heavy responsibility. There's no getting around the Lord's sobering words in Luke 12:48: *"From everyone who has been given much, much will be required; and to whom they entrusted much, of him they will ask all the more."*

Several principles of faithfulness are important to understand.

Faithful with it all

As followers of Christ, we need to be faithful in handling *all* of the money entrusted to us. Typically, Christians have been taught how to handle only ten percent of their income – the area of giving. While this is crucial, we rarely talk about our God-given responsibilities for the remaining 90 percent. Because of this, most of us know a lot more about the world's perspective on money than our Lord's perspective.

As a consequence of not being equipped to handle money biblically, many Christians develop wrong or distorted attitudes toward possessions which lead them to make some unwise financial decisions. Hosea 4:6 tells us, *"My people are destroyed for lack of knowledge."* Ignorance or disobedience of scriptural financial principles frequently slides into suffocating materialism, fractured relationships, and even money problems.

As followers of Christ we need to faithfully handle all of the money entrusted to us."

Unfaithful not entrusted with more

"There was a rich man who had a manager, and this manager was reported to him as squandering his possessions. And he called him and said to him, 'What is this I hear about you? Give an account of your management, for you can no longer be manager'" (Luke 16:1-2).

Two relevant principles emerge from this passage. First, wasting our possessions becomes public knowledge and creates a poor testimony. *"This manager was reported to him as squandering his possessions."* Second, the Lord will sometimes remove us as steward if we squander what He has given us.

In just three years a young entrepreneur earned a small fortune after founding a technology company. Then he went on an uncontrolled spending spree. Two years later he informed his staff that he had little left and everyone would need to economize. Shortly thereafter, he left for an expensive European vacation and had his office, already lavishly decorated, completely renovated.

I visited his office during his vacation, and his staff was laughing over his spending habits. I left with the distinct impression that the Lord would soon remove this man from stewardship over much, and He did. If you waste the possessions entrusted to you, the Lord may not choose to give you more.

Faithful in little things

How do you know if your son will take good care of his first car? Observe how he cared for his bicycle! How do you know if a salesperson will do a competent job of serving a large client? Evaluate how she served a small one. If we have the character to be faithful with small things, the Lord knows He can trust us with greater responsibilities. *"He who is faithful in a very little thing is faithful also in much . . ."* (Luke 16:10).

Almost every significant enterprise started out small. Apple founders Steve Jobs and Steve Wozniak tinkered with a personal computer in their garage. Sam Walton's first store was a small five-and-dime store in Bentonville, Arkansas before he built the Wal-Mart company. As they were faithful with small things, they were given greater responsibilities. Think of the origin of your wealth. Who was faithful with small things?

Missionary pioneer Hudson Taylor said it this way, "Small things are small things, but faithfulness with a small thing is a big thing."

LET THE ADVENTURE BEGIN

From God's perspective, leaving a legacy is far more than just leaving a heritage to your family for a few generations. In this book, you'll explore how you can finish well and leave a legacy that not only touches your family, but also influences families around the globe—and create an impact that will last forever.

You will wrestle with issues such as:

- Is God pleased with how I use my resources?

- How much is enough?

- How much do I leave my children and grandchildren?

- What limits should I set on my lifestyle?

- How can I learn to be content?

- How can I most effectively train my children to handle money?

- How much should I give?

- How do I deal with the relational impact wealth has on my family and friends?

- Why do I have a nagging sense of guilt that perhaps I am not doing enough good with my wealth?

- Are we handling debt wisely?

- Does my spouse understand our finances? Is he or she prepared to handle our business or finances in the event of my death?

- What do I do to leave a legacy to my children and grandchildren of walking closely with Christ and handling money God's way?

- Do I really know what God is calling me to do with my life and resources?

- How can I finish my life well?

In this book, you will be encouraged and challenged as you discover God's perspective on money. These timeless truths will help you get a fix on your position and enable you to plot a life course. In doing so, you will discover a greater measure of contentment, confidence that you are in God's will, and the joy of making an eternal difference.

A little history

In 1974, my business partner, Jim Seneff, challenged me to join him in a study of Scripture to discover what the Lord said about handling money. We read the entire Bible and were surprised to learn just how much it says about finances. We identified 2,350 verses and categorized them according to their topics. Learning and applying these principles had a profound impact on our personal finances and business careers.

That study literally changed the course of my life.

In 1983, my wife, Bev, and I finished developing an office complex that ultimately allowed us to become financially free. As a result, I have been able to serve full-time as a volunteer, teaching what the Bible says about handling money. The Lord had me found Crown Ministries, which merged with the ministry started by Larry Burkett to form Crown Financial Ministries. In 2009, the Lord prompted me to launch Compass—*finances God's way*.

I've had the privilege of leading more than 85 financial small group studies. In one of those groups everyone had a net worth of several million dollars. As time went on, it became clear to me that the issues these participants were grappling with differed from those of average income earners. In the environment of the small group, the participants developed very close relationships. Because the discussions were confidential, they became candid with the issues and struggles they were facing.

We assembled a focus group to help develop this book. Some in the group were entrepreneurs who made their money, others inherited money, and still others married into a wealthy family. There were also wealth managers and an extraordinarily capable widow. The focus group met over two-and-a-half years and conducted countless pilot studies to produce a small group study and this *Charting Your Legacy* book.

PERSONAL REFLECTIONS

- When you think of your own possessions and resources, what are your greatest struggles?

- What would you like to see happen in your life as a result of reading this book?

4

PERSPECTIVE

Warning! The next three chapters will challenge your thinking, your assumptions, and maybe some of your emotions!

I want you to remember that God, the Lord of heaven, loves you deeply. He isn't angry, surprised, or disappointed that you have significant resources. On the contrary, He has deliberately entrusted them to your care and management. Money is not evil; when used properly it can be a wonderful blessing. The following three chapters will help you understand the Lord's view of wealth and the unique challenges wealth poses to our relationship with Him.

GOD'S PERSPECTIVE ON WEALTH

Riches are meaningless apart from the Lord.

King Solomon had an annual income of more than $50 million. He lived in a palace that took thirteen years to build, owned 40,000 stalls of horses, sat on an ivory throne overlaid with gold, and drank from solid gold cups. The daily menu of his household included 100 sheep and 30 oxen. He became the very definition of a rich and powerful king.

Obviously, Solomon was in a position to evaluate whether the accumulation of money and possessions would bring true fulfillment. Here's his conclusion:

> "*I undertook great projects: I built houses for myself and planted vineyards. I made gardens and parks and planted all kinds of fruit trees in them. I made reservoirs to water groves of flourishing trees. I bought male and female slaves and had other slaves who were born in my house. I also owned more herds and flocks than anyone in Jerusalem before me. I amassed silver and gold for myself, and the treasure of kings and provinces. I acquired men and women singers, and a harem as well — the delights of the heart of man. I became greater by far than anyone in Jerusalem before me . . . Yet when I surveyed all that my hands had done and what I had toiled to achieve, everything was meaningless, a chasing after the wind*" (Ecclesiastes 2:4-11, NIV).

Nothing, even spectacular success, can replace the value of our relationship with the Lord. Ask yourself this question: Am I sacrificing an intimate relationship with Christ by focusing too much on growing my wealth or trusting in it? *"For what does it profit a man to gain the whole world, and forfeit his soul?"* (Mark 8:36).

Riches Are Uncertain.

A Florida real estate developer started from scratch and became one of the most successful in the state. His net worth grew to hundreds of millions of dollars. He and his family were admired, enjoyed wide influence among his peers, and had a reputation for generosity. A mountain of excessive debt, however, encumbered his real estate holdings. When the market turned sour, he lost all but a small portion of his assets.

His son later told me, "My father experienced humiliation and deep depression from which he has never recovered. His identity and significance as a person were tied to his success. Because of his humble beginnings, he had sworn that he never wanted to be dependent upon anyone, even his family. His financial statement became his security, and he grew accustomed to doing what he wanted when he wanted. Some of his most painful experiences were the embarrassment he felt when meeting his former friends. He used to enjoy being with people; now he avoids them."

Surveys have found that one of the most common fears among the wealthy is that of losing their wealth. This is one of the reasons there were so many suicides during the Great Depression. The Lord wants us to realize that riches are *uncertain*.

- *"Instruct those who are rich in this present world not to . . . fix their hope on the uncertainty of riches, but on God"* (1 Timothy 6:17).

- *Do not weary yourself to gain wealth, cease from your consideration of it. When you set your eyes on it, it is gone. For wealth certainly makes itself wings like an eagle that flies toward the heavens"* (Proverbs 23:4-5).

The only true certainty in life is the Lord Himself. He is forever faithful and worthy of our complete trust.

Riches are deceitful.

Riches are deceitful because they are tangible, and can blind us from the reality of the unseen Lord. On the surface, wealth seems to be able to do things that only Christ can really do: provide for needs, achieve happiness, and gain control of circumstances. *"And the one on whom seed was sown among the thorns, this is the man who hears the word, and the worry of the world, and the deceitfulness of wealth choke the word, and it becomes unfruitful"* (Matthew 13:22).

Riches are viewed differently by God.

Have you ever felt that "if only" you were in a more prestigious position – or had even more money – you could accomplish really significant things for the Lord? Let's examine two men who lived in Rome and who were at different ends of the economic spectrum.

In the coliseum, everyone stood waiting for Caesar before the gladiator contests were permitted to begin. When Caesar arrived, he was greeted with thunderous shouts of "Hail Caesar!" He had more power, prestige, and wealth than anyone else living at that time. He was worshipped as though he were a god.

In a different part of Rome another man lived in much different circumstances. Chained to guards in his prison cell, he invested his time praying and writing to a few of his friends. His name was Paul.

St. Paul in Prison, 1627 - Rembrandt

One man lived in an opulent palace; the other lived in a dingy cell. One had almost unlimited wealth; the other had almost nothing. One was the center of attention; the other was virtually ignored. Almost 2,000 years later, people around the world recognize which of these two men made the eternally important contribution. They name their children after the prisoner and their salads after the emperor!

God's perspective on true riches radically differs from that of most people. Let's unpack what the Lord said to the church in Laodicea in Revelation 3:15-19.

- First, the Laodiceans thought themselves wealthy, proudly self-sufficient, and without any real need to depend upon Christ. God saw them in an entirely different light – wretched, pitiful, poor, blind and naked. *"You say, 'I am rich; I have acquired wealth and do not need a thing.' But you do not realize that you are wretched, pitiful, poor, blind and naked"* (Revelation 3:17, NIV).

- Second, God assessed their commitment to Him and described it as lukewarm. Tepid! The consequences were frightening. The Lord was poised to spit – literally, vomit – them out of His mouth! *"I know your deeds, that you are neither cold nor hot . . . so because you are lukewarm, and neither hot nor cold, I will spit you out of My mouth"* (Revelation 3:15-16).

- Third, the Lord's advice to the Laodiceans was clear. Because your commitment to Christ is lukewarm and your wealth has blinded you to your constant need for Christ, I will discipline you unless you genuinely change. *"I counsel you to buy from me gold refined in the fire, so you can become rich; and white clothes to wear, so you can cover your shameful nakedness; and salve to put on your eyes, so you can see. Those whom I love I rebuke and discipline. So be earnest, and repent"* (Revelation 3:18-19, NIV).

In contrast to the Laodiceans, God said to the suffering church at Smyrna, *"I know your tribulation and your poverty (but you are rich)"* (Revelation 2:9). They were serious about following Christ and depending upon Him regardless of hardships, heartbreaks, and financial challenges. And here we are, twenty centuries later, still reading about the Lord's high regard for them.

✐ PERSONAL REFLECTIONS

- As you consider God's perspective of money and possessions, how does this influence your thinking?

5

DANGERS
OF WEALTH

Before we examine the dangers associated with being entrusted with much, it's important to answer the questions: *Am I rich? Am I at risk of these dangers?*

In our research, we discovered that many wealthy people don't *feel* rich because of the tendency to compare themselves with their peers. We all conduct both upward and downward comparisons. We tend to make upward comparisons with individuals who appear to have more than we do, and downward comparisons with those who have less.

Most of us spend more time conducting upward comparisons. Because of this, nearly all of us view our finances through a distorted lens, as depicted in the graphic on the next page. The left-hand side of the graphic illustrates how we feel about our finances when we compare ourselves to those who are richer. The right-hand side of the graphic portrays how we view our finances when we compare ourselves to those who are poorer. In almost all cases we *think* we are less well off than we *actually are.*[2]

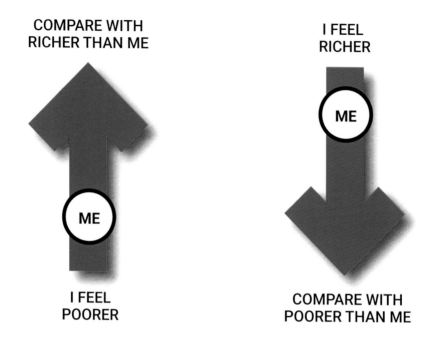

COMPARE WITH
RICHER THAN ME

I FEEL
RICHER

ME

ME

I FEEL
POORER

COMPARE WITH
POORER THAN ME

To help you more accurately assess whether you are rich, answer these questions:

On a scale of 1 to 10 (with 10 being the highest), how does your income and your net worth compare to the other seven billion people alive today?

On a scale of 1 to 10 (with 10 being the highest) how does your lifestyle – housing, transportation, food, clothing, recreation, entertainment, medical treatment and travel – compare with most people that have lived during the past 4,000 years?

In light of my answers, am I rich?

Scripture identifies several dangers associated with wealth and possessions. These are intended to protect you from harm on your spiritual journey. Review these thoughtfully and ask the Lord to make you aware of any dangers that might be nearer to your doorstep than you think.

Wealth tends to create pride.

Reflect on the way some wealthy people treat those who serve them. Have you ever detected an air of haughty impatience? It's good for all of us to remember that it is the Lord Himself who gives us success, skills, the power to create resources, and the keys to open doors of opportunity. The bottom line? We really have no room for pride based on our net worth. The following passages are just a sampling of many that tackle this issue head on.

- *"By your great wisdom, by your trade you have increased your riches and your heart is lifted up because of your riches"* (Ezekiel 28:5).

- *"Instruct those who are rich in this present world not to be conceited"* (1 Timothy 6:17).

- *". . . Let not a rich man boast of his riches; but let him who boasts boast of this, that he understands and knows Me"* (Jeremiah 9:23-24).

Pride renders us spiritually fruitless.

The only time we can be spiritually productive is when we are submitted to Jesus Christ as Lord and invite Him to live His life through us. Jesus said, *"I am the vine, you are the branches; he who abides in Me, and I in him, he bears much fruit; **for apart from Me you can do nothing**"* (John 15:5, emphasis added). Any time we are acting out of pride (the Bible also calls this the flesh), we are not yielded to Christ and are incapable of doing anything truly productive for God's kingdom. The apostle Paul expresses it this way in Galatians 2:20.

> *"I have been crucified with Christ and I no longer live, but Christ lives in me. The life I now live in the body, I live by faith in the Son of God, who loved me and gave himself for me"* (NIV).

In one of the more startling New Testament passages, the Lord actually declares Himself to be *opposed* to those who are proud. Opposed! By God Himself? I can't think of anything more terrifying than to be opposed by the almighty Creator of the universe. *". . . All of you, clothe yourselves with humility toward one another, for God is opposed to the proud, but gives grace to the humble"* (1 Peter 5:5). Proverbs 16:5 adds, *"The Lord detests **all the proud**"* *of heart"* (NIV, emphasis added). We are commanded to do nothing out of pride, but to rather act with gracious humility toward others.

The sin of pride undermines our relationship with the Lord and other people, rendering us spiritually ineffective. No wonder our loving heavenly Father warns us so strongly against this attitude!

Pride is spiritual cancer: it eats up the very possibility of love, or contentment, or even common sense." – C.S. Lewis

We tend to trust in wealth.

Let's face it, it is ever-so-easy for us to trust in our assets. Ever so slowly, they can become our god. We tend to trust in that which we can see with our eyes, rather than in the invisible living God.

- *"Instruct those who are rich in this present world not . . . to fix their hope on the uncertainty of riches, but on God, who richly supplies us with all things to enjoy"* (1 Timothy 6:17).

- *"For when I bring them into the land flowing with milk and honey, which I swore to their fathers, and they have eaten and are satisfied and become prosperous, then they will turn to other gods and serve them, and spurn Me and break My covenant"* (Deuteronomy 31:20).

Someone once observed, "For every ninety-nine who can be poor and remain close to Christ, only one can become wealthy and maintain close fellowship with Him." Those aren't very good odds, are they? We cling tightly to the Lord when we are totally dependent on Him to provide for our needs. Once we have resources and become more self-sufficient, however, we often take the Lord for granted, believing we don't need Him as much.

A father was carrying his two-year-old son as he waded in a lake. While they were close to shore, the child was unconcerned because of the apparent safety of the beach – even though the water was deep enough to drown him. He didn't understand his absolute dependence upon his father. The farther they moved away from shore, however, the more tightly the boy clung to his dad.

Like the little boy, we are at all times completely dependent upon the Lord's provision. Apart from Him, we couldn't even draw our next breath. The truth is, however, we often don't recognize our dependence when we are "close to shore," experiencing the apparent security of financial prosperity. Candidly, this has been a struggle for me as well. It's easy for me to start leaning on my financial assets – without realizing that they are subtly replacing my confidence in Christ. Knowing that money can buy goods, services, and the best health care on the market, my natural tendency is to trust in that which I can see, rather than in the invisible living God. My natural tendency is to first look to my money to solve problems, instead of first praying and seeking the Lord.

Proverbs 18:10-11 draws an interesting contrast between the righteous and the rich. The passage says, *"The name of the LORD is a fortified tower; the righteous run to it and are safe. The wealth of the rich is their fortified city; they imagine it a wall too high to scale"* (NIV). The contrast is not between the righteous and the rich in an absolute sense, as there are many people who are both righteous and wealthy. Rather, the contrast is drawn between the two primary objects of man's trust: God and money. Those who trust in the Lord are safe; those who trust in wealth only imagine that they are safe.[2]

Riches and abundance come clad in sheep's clothing pretending to be security against anxieties, and they instead become the object of anxiety." – Richard Foster

Partiality

Another danger is partiality. Consider James 2:1-9, *"Do not hold your faith in our glorious Lord Jesus Christ with an attitude of personal favoritism. For if a man comes into your assembly with a gold ring and dressed in fine clothes, and there also comes in a poor man in dirty clothes, and you pay special attention to the one who is wearing the fine clothes . . . have you not made distinctions among yourselves, and become judges with **evil motives?** . . . **if you show partiality, you are committing sin and are convicted by the law as transgressors"** (emphasis added). Partiality doesn't have to be based on a person's wealth; it can also grow out of a person's education or social position.

How do we break the habit of partiality? Romans 12:10 tells us, *"Be devoted to one another in brotherly love; give preference to one another in honor."* Philippians 2:3 reads, *". . . With humility of mind regard one another as more important than yourselves."* We need to ask the Lord to ingrain in our thinking the habit of elevating each person, regardless of his or her station in life, as more important than ourselves.

One practical way to overcome partiality is to concentrate on the strengths and abilities of each person. Understanding that every person can do some things better than I can helps me appreciate all people.

The Desire to Be Rich

Scripture also warns against the desire for greater riches. The purpose of this principle can be difficult to understand. The Bible doesn't say that it's wrong to become rich. In fact, I believe God delights in prospering a man or woman who has been focused on becoming a faithful steward. **There is nothing wrong with becoming wealthy if it is a by-product of being a faithful steward.** The central issue here is a person's attitude toward material gain. In 1 Timothy 6:9, Paul wrote,

> *"Those who want to get rich fall into temptation and a snare and many foolish and harmful desires which plunge men into ruin and destruction."*

Study these words carefully. The text doesn't say **most** of those who want to get rich; it says, plainly, "those who want to get rich." In other words, **everyone** who wants to get rich will *"fall into temptation and a snare and* *many foolish and harmful desires which plunge men into ruin and destruction."* Everyone!

For much of my life I wanted to become super rich, so you can imagine the difficulty I faced in dealing with this truth. When I want to get rich, I am self-centered and motivated by pride, greed, or an unhealthy compulsion to prepare for survival in an uncertain economic future. But when I simply desire to be a faithful steward, I am Christ-centered in my thinking; my actions are motivated from a pure heart. I am serving Christ, and I am growing closer to Him.

The next verse reveals another reason our Lord warns against pursuing riches.

> *"For the love of money is a root of all sorts of evil, and some by longing for it have wandered away from the faith and pierced themselves with many griefs"* (1 Timothy 6:10).

When we want to get rich, Scripture tells us that we love money. In Matthew 6:24 we read, *"No one can serve two masters, for either he will hate the one and love the other, or he will be devoted to the one and despise the other. You cannot serve God and Money."*

When we are captivated by wanting to get rich, we are actually loving money and hating God. We are devoted to money and despising God. We are serving money, and we are not serving God. The end of 1 Timothy 6:10 reads, *"Some by longing for it* [riches] *have wandered away from the faith and pierced themselves with many griefs."* I have witnessed firsthand the truth of this Scripture. For years I greatly admired the man who introduced me to Christ. But sadly, as time went by, he drifted from his simple faith in Jesus. Although he was already wealthy, he became obsessed in his desire to grow even wealthier. Finally, he divorced his wife and abandoned his four young sons. He denied Christ repeatedly and wandered away from the faith. Wanting to get rich, which is the love of money, is a devastating spiritual condition to be in.

Flee and Submit

How can we overcome the strong temptation to multiply our wealth for the wrong reasons? By remembering to split and submit! In 1 Timothy 6:11, Paul counsels Timothy to *"Flee from these things* [the desire to get rich], *you man of God, and pursue righteousness, godliness, faith, love, perseverance and gentleness."*

When you become aware of your desire to increase your riches for the wrong reason, *run* from that temptation and replace it with a godly pursuit.

Next, submit. The ultimate way of escape is submitting to Jesus as Lord. We can do this in confidence, because Jesus overcame a massive temptation to become fantastically rich. After Christ fasted forty days in the wilderness, the devil tempted Him three times. The final temptation is recorded in Luke 4:5-7, *"And he* [the devil] *led* [Jesus] *up and showed Him all the kingdoms of the world in a moment of time. And the devil said to Him, 'I will give You all this domain and its glory . . . if You worship me.'"* Can you imagine that temptation? In an instant, Jesus was shown all the kingdoms of the world. However, because He was submitted entirely to the Father and was empowered by the same Holy Spirit who lives in us, He was able to resist the temptation.

I am of the opinion that our heavenly Father is far *less* likely to increase our resources when we are motivated simply to get rich. Wanting more – loving money – closely parallels greed. And *"greed . . . amounts to idolatry"* (Colossians 3:5). The Father watches jealously over His children to ensure that we will not be drawn away from loving Him with all our hearts.

✏ PERSONAL REFLECTIONS

- The Bible tells us that possessing wealth tends to create pride. How do you plan to overcome this?

Read 1 Timothy 6:17 *"Instruct those who are rich in this present world not . . . to fix their hope on the uncertainty of riches, but on God, who richly supplies us with all things to enjoy."*

- What does this verse say to you and how will you implement it?

RECOMMENDED RESOURCES

Humility by Andrew Murray. Published by Bethany House Publishers. This book is a must-read classic for those who are serious about growing deeper in their relationship with Christ. An audio version is also available on YouTube.

6

LIFESTYLE

One of the biggest challenges of living in a consumer society is simply determining the lifestyle the Lord wants for us. No matter what you may have heard, the Bible nowhere prescribes one standard of living for everyone. In Scripture, godly people are represented in all walks of life, and to this day the Lord still continues to place His people strategically in every level of society – rich and poor and everywhere in between.

Ask the Lord to help you evaluate and even wrestle (in a healthy way) with your standard of living. To stimulate your thinking, let's examine several principles that should influence your lifestyle.

Learn to be content.

The word "contentment" is mentioned six times in Scripture – and five of those times it has to do with money. Paul wrote,

> "I have learned to be content in whatever circumstances I am. I know how to get along with humble means, and I also know how to live in prosperity; in any and every circumstance I have learned the secret of being filled and going hungry, both of having abundance and suffering need. I can do all things through Him who strengthens me" (Philippians 4:11-13).

Read through this passage more than once, noting that Paul "learned" to be content. Contentment isn't something we're born with; it is something we *learn*. There are two elements to contentment:

- Know how God wants you to handle the assets He has entrusted to you.

- Be faithful to do what He wants with them.

Note carefully that it's not just *knowing* these things that brings contentment; it is *doing* them. As author Francis Schaeffer said, "These two words, know and do, occur throughout Scripture and always in that order. We cannot do until we know, but we can know without doing. The house built on the rock is the house of the man who knows and does. The house built on the sand is the house of the man who knows but does not do."

These two words, know and do, occur throughout Scripture and always in that order. We cannot do until we know, but we can know without doing." – Francis Schaeffer

Once we have been faithful in the doing, we can be content in knowing that our loving heavenly Father will entrust us with the precise possessions He knows will be best for us at any particular time.

We should never equate biblical contentment with laziness, social insensitivity, or apathy. Because we serve the living and dynamic God, Christians should always be improving, growing, and "pressing on toward the goal," as Paul put it in Philippians 3:14. And don't imagine that contentment somehow cancels out properly motivated ambition. I believe that we should have the burning desire to be increasingly faithful stewards of the talents and possessions He has entrusted to us.

Biblical contentment is an inner peace that accepts what God has chosen for our present vocation, station in life, and financial state. Hebrews 13:5 emphasizes this: *"Make sure your character is free from the love of money, being content with what you have; for He Himself has said, 'I will never desert you, nor will I ever forsake you.'"*

Freely enjoy whatever you spend in the "Spirit."

Prayerfully submit spending decisions to the Lord. Seeking the Lord's direction in spending does not mean that we will never spend for anything other than a basic necessity. During the Christmas season several years ago, my wife asked me to purchase a gift that I considered extravagant. I did promise, however, to seek the Lord's direction. As we prayed, He made it clear that we should purchase the item, which we have thoroughly enjoyed and appreciated. *"For everything created by God is good, and nothing is to be rejected if it is received with gratitude"* (1 Timothy 4:4). Study the last part of 1 Timothy 6:17: *"God, who richly supplies us with all things to enjoy."*

We aren't to feel guilty when the Lord gives us the freedom to buy something. Remember, the Lord has entrusted you with assets. You're responsible for managing this wealth in a way that pleases Him. The Lord has given you freedom to spend, but not license to spend carelessly.

When you consider a purchase, ask yourself why you want it. Is it a healthy pleasure, or are you just trying to impress others? How will it help you reach your life goals? As with everything else in life, seek God's direction. Listen to His words to the prophet Isaiah: *"I am the LORD your God, who teaches you what is best for you, who directs you in the way you should go"* (Isaiah 48:17, NIV).

Influence of comparison

Jonathan and Vivian thoroughly enjoyed spending July and August in the North Carolina mountains to get relief from hot Florida summers. They had inherited their modest mountain home from Vivian's parents – a home filled with memories of her family vacationing there. As they started their car to visit some old college friends they hadn't seen in years, they talked about God's goodness in providing this second home. They were grateful. They were content.

Thirty minutes later, they pulled into the driveway of their friends. Jonathan's curiosity about how his MBA classmate had fared was answered immediately. The lawn was manicured. The house and the furnishings were stunning. The view from the mountain top was magnificent.

The drive home felt depressing. The gratitude they had experienced just a few hours before had faded, like sunlight swallowed up by a dark cloud. Just that quickly, they had become discontent.

What happened? How can our hearts transition so quickly from gratitude to discontentment? The answer – in a word – is *comparison*. Comparison typically changes the focus from enjoying what we have to obsessing over what we lack.

Comparison is a thief because it steals gratitude and contentment from us.[3] Comparison is a killer because it can destroy a heart that is thankful to God for His provision and replace it with a heart that covets—and edges toward raw idolatry.

> *"But immorality or any impurity or greed must not even be named among you, as is proper among saints . . . this you know with certainty, that no immoral or impure person or* **covetous man, who is an idolater***, has an inheritance in the kingdom of Christ and God"* (Ephesians 5:3, 5, emphasis added).

Influence of advertising

Romans 12:2 begins with this command, *"Do not be conformed to this world."* The Amplified version reads this way: *"Do not be conformed to this world – this age, fashioned after and adapted to its external, superficial customs"* (Romans 12:2, AMPC).

We live in one of the most affluent cultures the world has ever known. Day in and day out, night in and night out, we are bombarded with manipulative, highly effective advertising. The purpose of advertising, of course, is to motivate us to spend money. Ads usually stress the importance of image rather than function. For example, automobile ads rarely focus on a car as reliable transportation that is economical to operate. Instead, they project an image of status or sex appeal. Reflect on the claims of TV commercials.

No matter what the product – clothing, deodorants, credit cards, cars, beverages, the list goes on and on – the underlying message insists that the "fulfilling, beautiful, wrinkle-free life" can be ours if we are willing to buy it.

We would be less than honest to deny the influence of this media onslaught on our attitudes and our lives. Author George Fooshee so aptly states, "People buy things they do not need to impress people they do not even like."

None of us is immune to the lure of this message. From time to time we all get hooked on something we think we must buy – a new car, second home, airplane, the latest smartphone – you name it. Once hooked, it is very easy to rationalize the purchase of anything. When facing a major decision, seek the Lord's guidance and the counsel of godly people who will help you ask the hard questions.

Why do the wicked prosper?

This is a disturbing question God's people have asked for centuries. If we allow ourselves to be caught up in that line of questioning, it can lead us down a path of discontentment—just as it has for multitudes of others through the years. The prophet Jeremiah inquired of the Lord: *"You are always righteous, LORD, when I bring a case before you. Yet I would speak with you about your justice: Why does the way of the wicked prosper?"* (Jeremiah 12:1, NIV).

The author of Psalm 73 also asked why the wicked prospered, and frankly admitted being envious of them. Then the Lord revealed the wicked person's end – sudden eternal punishment.

"Surely God is good to . . . those who are pure in heart. But as for me, my feet had almost slipped . . . for I envied the arrogant when I saw the prosperity of the wicked. . . When I tried to understand all this, it troubled me deeply till I entered the sanctuary of God; then I understood their final destiny. Surely you place them on slippery ground; you cast them down to ruin. How suddenly are they destroyed, completely swept away by terrors!" (Psalm 73:1-19, NIV).

The Bible tells us that although some of the wicked will certainly prosper, we are not to envy them, because their life on earth is short. *"Do not fret because of those who are evil or be envious of those who do wrong; for like the grass they will soon wither, like green plants they will soon die away"* (Psalm 37:1-2, NIV).

Consider living more simply.

Many who are wealthy live busy, over-committed lives, making choices that only multiply their busyness. Possessions require time, attention, and money to maintain. Certain possessions and investments can demand so much that they distract us from our relationship with the Lord and our family. An admirer asked the owner of a large dairy farm how many cattle he owned. The farmer shook his head and responded, "I don't own them, they own me. I'm up at 4:30 every morning because they demand to be milked." What was true of the dairyman is often true of us.

Study this verse: *"In the presence of the LORD is fullness of joy"* (Psalm 16:11). Do you want to live in fullness of joy? Then nurture your fellowship with Christ. Enjoy His companionship. Make decisions that will facilitate rather than distract from entering His presence. The less complicated our lives become, the better we are able to invest ourselves in nurturing our relationship with the Lord and building His kingdom. *"Make it your ambition to lead a quiet life and attend to your own business"* (1 Thessalonians 4:11).

Review your assets and business interests. Make a list of your commitments that require time. Carefully evaluate them. How can you restructure them so that they will require less time? How can you simplify?

It's also important to consider *all* the impacts a decision can have on you and your family. Consider the large vacation home that caught the eye of George and Janet Connor. They purchased it. "After all," they reasoned, "we have five young children who will enjoy it. And we can let pastors and missionaries use it as a retreat when we're not there." After purchasing the home, they felt compelled to use it most weekends because of their significant investment in the property. The family attended church less frequently, and they lost contact with many of their close friends. Their lifestyle became more leisure oriented, and they gradually lost the desire to be involved in the things of God. Later they discovered that when their children became teenagers, the children preferred to be involved with their own friends rather than with the family. And few pastors ever used the vacation home. Please think through major, life-altering decisions such as vacation homes.

"

The purpose of reducing a busy expensive lifestyle, is increasing our available time, energy, and resources for that which is eternally important." – Brandon Sieben, CEO, Compass – *Finances God's Way*

Develop a wartime mentality.

Imagine for a moment that you're a British civilian during World War II. Western Europe has fallen to the Nazis and on July 10, 1940, the Battle of Britain begins. German airplanes and bombs continue to hammer London, and all England is focused on one thing: winning the war.

Everyone sacrifices. People plant victory gardens and drive at the "victory-speed" of 35 miles an hour. Materials needed for the war are carefully rationed. Everyone commits their time and resources to this one cause.

As author John Piper observed: "[A wartime mindset] tells me that there is a war going on in the world between Christ and Satan, truth and falsehood, belief and unbelief. It tells me there are soldiers and weapons to be funded. It tells me that the stakes of this conflict are higher than any other war in history. They are eternal and infinite: heaven or hell, eternal joy or eternal torment.

"I need to hear this message again and again, because I drift into a peace-time mindset. Before you know it, I am using my money just the way those who don't know Christ do. I begin to forget about the war. I don't think much about people perishing."

He is right! It is easy to be blinded in our consumer culture to the reality of the unseen spiritual war. Of course, even in war, rest and leisure are proper and needed. Hobbies, sports, and vacations are all appropriate and should be enjoyed to the full. But we need to establish our lifestyle and our spending in light of eternity.

So here's a question to pray about before answering. Has it really dawned on you that – right now – you are in the most important war in all of history? People around the world have been swept up into this battle with eternal destinies at stake. Do your lifestyle and the investment of your energy and resources reflect that reality? To what extent are you focused on helping men and women know and grow in Jesus Christ?

✏️ PERSONAL REFLECTIONS

View the video – God is every part of your life – Jess and Angela Correll (9:21) on ChartingYourLegacy.org, or by using this QR code.

- What part of their story impacted you the most and why?

- Write a description of your current lifestyle (with your spouse, if you are married).

- If you sense that the Lord would have you alter any part of it, describe what those changes might be.

- Who will you ask to hold you accountable for these changes?

RECOMMENDED RESOURCES

God and Money: How We Discovered True Riches at Harvard Business School by John Cortines and Gregory Baumer. Published by Rose Publishing. An outstanding and motivating book written by two Harvard Business School graduates. It wonderfully addresses issues such as lifestyle and spending limits.

Satisfied: Discovering Contentment in a World of Consumption by Jeff Manion. Published by Zondervan Publishers. A winsome but powerful book that will help you identify how our culture is robbing us of the joy and contentment the Lord intends for us to enjoy.

7

CRISIS

S tarting from scratch, the three Schrimsher brothers built a highly respected real estate investment company in Florida. For thirty years, Steve, Frank, and Michael operated their business based squarely on biblical principles: hard work, integrity, and a commitment to eliminate personal and business debt. The business thrived.

Everything changed on June 25, 2008. Without warning, their largest joint-venture partner committed suicide. Shockingly, over the weeks that followed, they discovered that he had embezzled and largely spent more than 33 million dollars from their partnerships!

It was front page news, and the Schrimshers – faced with the need to finish major half-completed apartment projects owned by defrauded investors – were unsure if their business would even survive. Even though their reputation had been severely damaged and they were threatened with lawsuits from panicked investors, the brothers determined to over-communicate with their investors. They remained fully transparent even when the news was bad.

During one particularly discouraging time, Steve's wife told him, "We started with nothing, and if we lose everything, we still have each other. More importantly, we still have Christ."

The brothers decided, "All we can do is to get up every morning and do the next right thing, no matter what." They prayed that the Lord would honor their faithfulness and hard work, and He has been gracious to do just that.

Unexpectedly, two large insurance policies covering their development partner's life were assigned to them to pay back about 40 percent of the stolen money. Subsequently, several projects were completed and sold, allowing them to recover even more of the money.

To date, about two-thirds of the money has been returned to the investors. The Schrimshers remain committed to do all they can to return every penny that was lost. Amazingly, their reputation is better today than it was before they learned of the embezzlement!

A friend once told me, half in jest, "Everyone goes through crises. You've either just come out of one, you're in the middle of one, or you're just about to go into one – you just don't know it yet!"

Some challenges build slowly and can be anticipated; others appear without warning. Some are resolved quickly; others are chronic. Some reflect the consequences of our actions; others are completely beyond our control. Some crises impact an entire nation; others are isolated to us as individuals. The death of a family member, a serious health issue, a fractured relationship with someone close, a financial challenge – these and a host of other serious crises can shake us to the core.

For many of those entrusted with significant resources, a crisis can be particularly difficult. Why? Because they are used to being able to solve most of their problems with the stroke of a pen.

I call these challenges the "storms of life." While some of the storms amount to little more than a blustery rain shower, others feel like a category-five hurricane.

Please remember this one thing: No matter the crisis, you don't face it alone. Put yourself in the sandals of a few of God's people in the Bible who faced dark and terrifying category-five storms.

- Job, in a matter of just a few hours, lost his children, his financial resources, the respect of his closest friends, and finally his health.

- Joseph was sold into slavery and later cruelly slandered – just before he was thrown into prison.

- Moses and the children of Israel faced annihilation by Egypt's powerful army in a seemingly hopeless cul-de-sac at the Red Sea.

- Daniel was tossed into a den of hungry lions.

- Paul was beaten, stoned, and left for dead on his missionary journeys.

The list goes on and on.

Although storms are often emotional, scary, and painful, if we maintain God's perspective, we can survive – and even grow – through such dark days (and nights!).

GOD'S ROLE

When facing a crisis, *nothing* is more important than knowing who God is. That may be one of the most important statements in this book. We need Him, and we need to know Him – His love, care, control, and power. Only the Bible reveals the true extent of God's involvement in our challenges. If we have an inadequate or warped view of God and His purposes, then we won't fully embrace and learn from our challenges. What's more, we will forfeit the peace, contentment, and even joy that God makes available to us in the midst of the storm.

God loves you.

God's very nature is summed up in 1 John 4:8, *"God is love."* He loves you and remains intimately involved with you as an individual throughout your whole life. Consider Psalm 139:17-18, *"How precious it is, Lord, to realize that you are thinking about me constantly! I can't even count how many times a day your thoughts turn toward me"* (TLB).

In other words, as mind-boggling as this concept might be – the Creator of the universe never stops thinking about you!

Do you need further evidence of His love? Consider John 15:9 – which has to be one of the most encouraging verses in all the Bible. Jesus says: *"As the Father has loved me, so have I loved you"* (NIV).

Don't skim over those words!

Let the implications sink in for a moment.

Consider how much God the Father loves God the Son. They have existed *forever* in the closest possible relationship with a deep, unfathomable love for each other. And Jesus says THIS is how much He loves you! Could it be? Yes! We have Christ's own word on it.

In any crisis, it's critical to be reminded of God's unfailing love and faithfulness. Why? Because it's so very easy to become discouraged and lose hope. It's easy to forget God's love and care for you, especially when adversity first strikes – or goes on and on for what feels like an eternity.

Jeremiah the prophet was completely discouraged. He wrote: *"I remember my affliction and my wandering . . . my soul is downcast within me"* (Lamentations 3:19-20, NIV). But then he remembered the Lord. *"Yet this I call to mind and therefore I have hope: Because of the LORD's great love we are not consumed, for his compassions never fail. They are new every morning; great is your faithfulness"* (Lamentations 3:21-23, NIV).

It is helpful to meditate on passages such as these:

> *". . . God has said, 'Never will I leave you; never will I forsake you.'* *So we say with confidence, 'The Lord is my helper; I will not be afraid.* *What can mere mortals do to me?'"* (Hebrews 13:5-6, NIV).

> *"Who shall separate us from the love of Christ? Shall trouble or hardship or persecution or famine or nakedness or danger or sword? No, in*

all these things we are more than conquerors through him who loved us" (Romans 8:35, 37, NIV).

I've discovered that even in a crisis, the Lord will do kind, loving things that offer clear evidence of His care and concern. Consider Joseph. While a slave, *"[Joseph's] master saw that the LORD was with him"* (Genesis 39:3), so his master put him in charge of all he owned. Later in prison, *"the LORD was with Joseph and extended kindness to him, and gave him favor in the sight of the chief jailer"* (Genesis 39:21).

God is in control.

God is ultimately in control of every event. This is but a sampling of passages that affirm His control:

- *"We adore you as being in control of everything"* (1 Chronicles 29:11, TLB).

- *"Whatever the LORD pleases, He does, in heaven and in earth . . ."* (Psalm 135:6).

- *"For nothing will be impossible with God"* (Luke 1:37).

The Lord is in control even of difficult events. *"I am the LORD, and there is no other, the One forming light and creating darkness, causing well-being and creating calamity; I am the LORD who does all these"* (Isaiah 45:6-7).

GOD HAS A PURPOSE FOR ADVERSITY

The Cecropia moth emerges from its cocoon only after a long, exhausting struggle to free itself. A young boy, wishing to help the moth, carefully slit the exterior of the cocoon. Soon it came out, but its wings were shriveled and couldn't function. What the young boy didn't realize was that the moth's struggle to liberate itself from the cocoon was essential to the development of its wings and its ability to fly.

No struggle, no wings.[4]

Much like the cocoon of the moth, adversity has a part to play in our lives. God uses those difficult, sometimes heartbreaking times to mature us in Christ. James 1:2-4 says it this way: *"Consider it **pure joy**, my brothers* [and sisters], *whenever you face trials of many kinds, because you know that the testing of your faith produces perseverance. Let perseverance finish its work so that you may be mature and complete, not lacking anything"* (NIV, emphasis added).

Stop. Carefully read this passage again. Think about it. Whenever we are going through any type of difficulty, we are to consider it pure joy. Why? Because the Lord knows it can lead to a closer relationship with Him—and nothing is more valuable than that.

God designs challenging circumstances for our ultimate benefit. Romans 8:28-29 tells us, *"We know that in all things God works for the good of those who love him, who have been called according to his purpose. For those God foreknew he also predestined to be conformed to the image of his Son . . ."* (NIV). And the primary good that God works in our lives is to make us more like Christ.

We see this same thought expressed in Hebrews 12:6, 10-11, *"For those whom the Lord loves He disciplines . . . He disciplines us for our good, so that we may share His holiness. All discipline for the moment seems not to be joyful, but sorrowful; yet to those who have been trained by it, afterwards it yields the peaceful fruit of righteousness."* God makes no mistakes. He knows exactly what He wants us to become, and He also knows exactly what is necessary to produce that result in our lives.

Author Alan Redpath wrote, "There is nothing – no circumstances, no trouble, no testing – that can ever touch me until, first of all, it has gone past God, past Christ, right through to me. If it has come that far, it has come with great purpose, which I may not understand at the moment. But as I refuse to panic, as I lift my eyes to Him and accept it as coming from the throne of God for some great purpose of blessing to my own heart, no sorrow will ever disturb me, no trial will ever disarm me, no circumstance will cause me to fret, for I shall rest in the joy of what my Lord is."

If God subtracted one pain, one heartache, one disappointment from my life, I would be less than the person I am now, less the person wants me to be, and my ministry would be less than He intends." – Ron Dunn

Bev and I endured – and benefited from – many storms, from the birth and death of a precious special-needs child, to an unwanted career change, to Bev's double mastectomy to rid her of breast cancer that later spread to her bones and liver. Through the crucible of our pain and tears, many of the Bible's truths grew from wispy theory into rock-solid reality. Although we would never want to repeat these experiences, we are incredibly grateful for how the Lord used them in our lives.

Author Ron Dunn observed: "If God subtracted one pain, one heartache, one disappointment from my life, I would be less than the person I am now, less the person God wants me to be, and my ministry would be less than He intends."

Please don't miss this point. You and I need to recognize difficulties as opportunities to grow into the people God wants us to be. In adversity we learn things we just couldn't learn any other way.

I know what you're thinking: *Easy for you to say, Howard. You have no idea what we've been through.* Granted. But then, I could also say, "You have no idea what *we* have been through during our forty-six years of marriage." And yet the Lord Jesus has stood with us in every crisis, every heartache, every difficult decision. Every one of those incidents, painful though they were, brought us closer to Him and closer to each other.

You can be comforted knowing that your loving heavenly Father is in absolute control of every situation you will ever face. He intends to use each circumstance for a good purpose. First Thessalonians 5:18 says it well, *"Give* *thanks in **all** circumstances; for this is God's will for you in Christ Jesus*" (NIV, emphasis added).

Sometimes, even when we fully obey the Lord, we will experience a major crisis or heartbreak. Why? We often will have no idea how to answer that question. But we can be confident that the Lord will use all such challenges to fulfill His purposes. Luke 8:22-25 records such an example. *"Jesus said to his disciples, 'Let's go over to the other side of the lake.'. . . So they got into a boat and set out. As they sailed, he fell asleep. A squall came down on the lake, so that the boat was being swamped, and they were in great danger. The disciples went and woke him, saying, 'Master, Master, we're going to drown!' He got up and rebuked the wind and the raging waters; the storm subsided, and all was calm. 'Where is your faith?' he asked the disciples"* (NIV).

Christ in the storm by Rembrandt 1633

Consider this: The disciples did exactly what Jesus asked of them. Several of the disciples were seasoned fishermen who had surely spent thousands of hours fishing on this lake in all kinds of weather. When the unexpected squall swept across the water, they panicked, knowing all too well that their very lives were at risk.

After Jesus calmed the storm, He challenged the disciples about their lack of faith. In fact, His whole agenda had been to increase their faith by placing them in a life-threatening situation that only He could solve. And He solved it by simply commanding the storm to be calm.

Trust God.

We should view challenges and crises through the lens of God's love, faith-fulness, and control. The Bible makes it clear that God offers security only in Himself – not in business, not in money, not in a career, and not in other people. External things offer the illusion of security, but the Lord alone can be fully trusted. *"The LORD is good, a refuge in times of trouble. He cares for those who trust in him"* (Nahum 1:7, NIV). *"When I am afraid, I will put my trust in You. In God, whose word I praise, in God I have put my trust; I shall not be afraid . . ."* (Psalm 56:3-4).

✎ PERSONAL REFLECTIONS

- Why do you think it is important to realize that God loves you and is in control of the situation when you face a significant difficulty or a crisis?

- Think about a crisis you have experienced. How did the Lord ultimately use it in your life?

RECOMMENDED RESOURCE

Jerry Bridges, *Trusting God.* NavPress, 2008.

Some of the original concepts and examples in this chapter are from the excellent book, *Trusting God* by Jerry Bridges, NavPress, 2008. It is a classic. We recommend it without reservation.

IN THE EYE OF
THE STORM

What's the first question that comes to your mind when you face a gut-wrenching crisis?

Through the years, I've been close to many people in those situations. Generally, the first question they usually ask it, "How can I fix this? How can I solve this problem?"

Jesus answers the question this way in Matthew 7:24-25: *"Everyone who hears these words of mine and **puts them into practice** is like a wise man who built his house on the rock. The rain came down, the streams rose, and the winds blew and beat against that house; yet it did not fall, because it had its foundation on the rock"* (NIV, emphasis added).

Study this passage carefully. Picture the situation. The rain came down, the streams rose, and the winds blew and beat against the house. The storm came from every direction!

The key to solving most types of challenges is learning and practicing God's solution. It truly can be that simple. For example, when facing financial or business crises, learn what the Bible says about them.

When you finish this book, you will know much of God's framework for handling money. But *knowing* is only half of what you need. The other half is *applying* what you have learned. It may take a long time and a lot of effort to navigate a financial storm, but you will know the basics of what you should do.

James 1:22-25 bluntly emphasizes the importance of applying God's truth directly to our life situations:

> *"Do not merely listen to the word, and so deceive yourselves. **Do what it says.** Anyone who listens to the word but does not do what it says is like someone who looks at his face in a mirror and, after looking at himself, goes away and immediately forgets what he looks like. But whoever looks intently into the perfect law that gives freedom, and continues in it – not forgetting what they have heard, but doing it – they will be blessed in what they do"* (emphasis added, NIV).

Don't compromise or half-heartedly implement what the Lord has graciously revealed about your crisis. As the James passage instructs us – *"do what the Word says"* so that you will be blessed in what you do.

Part of what you'll learn in chapter 10 is God's desire for us to be generous givers. When facing a financial crisis, the tendency is to hold on tightly to what we have at the expense of our generosity. A passage in the book of Acts, however, shows us a different way. In Acts 11:28-29, we read: *"Agabus [a prophet] . . . through the Spirit predicted that a severe famine would spread over the entire Roman world. (This happened during the reign of Claudius.) The disciples, as each one was able, decided to provide help for the brothers and sisters living in Judea"* (NIV).

Consider this. The Holy Spirit revealed through a prophet that a severe world-wide famine was coming soon, and their first reaction was to get out their checkbooks! Don't allow a crisis to stop you from remaining generous. You may not be able to give as much as you did previously, but still give.

It's also important to quickly evaluate how the circumstance will impact your finances and to make the necessary adjustments for any diminished income or increased expenses. And if you are married, don't forget to communicate! Tell the Lord *and* tell your spouse your feelings and concerns. How important is this? It's important enough to schedule a time *every day* to talk, so you can encourage each other. Bev and I discovered that a challenging time or crisis doesn't have to damage our marriage; in fact, it can be a catalyst to improve it. I am fully persuaded that God intends married couples to grow closer together during a crisis rather than allow the difficulties to damage their marriage.

When you buy an expensive toy, such as an exotic second home, large boat, or plane, you must factor in ongoing costs. What seems inexpensive when things are going well can become intolerably expensive during an unexpected financial crisis."
– Todd Haag

Never go through a storm alone.

What I want to emphasize here is the importance of not going it alone. It is almost impossible to make wise decisions in isolation in the midst of a crisis. Seek advice from people who have been through similar situations. You will draw strength not only from their emotional support but also from their experience. There are people all around you who have weathered similar storms, and you can gain from their knowledge, discovering mistakes to avoid and resources to help. Ask your church and friends to pray; it's their most meaningful contribution.

King Solomon said it this way: *"Two can accomplish more than twice as much as one, for the results can be much better. If one falls, the other pulls him up; but if a man falls when he is alone, he's in trouble"* (Ecclesiastes 4:9-10, TLB).

Live one day at a time.

Roberto Menendez started and built an extraordinarily successful construction business. He was extremely generous and enjoyed a wonderful reputation. And then came the crushing financial crisis of 2008, crippling his business and pushing him to the brink of bankruptcy.

Roberto confided, "In a crisis, the tendency is to look ahead and become overwhelmed with all the problems. We are to plan ahead, but for our mental and emotional health we must follow what Jesus Christ told us: *Do not worry about tomorrow, for tomorrow will worry about itself. Each day has enough trouble of its own*" (Matthew 6:34, NIV).

Live focused on today! And if the crisis becomes overwhelming, focus on one moment at a time in close fellowship with Christ. And don't let anyone tell you that this is an "escape from reality." It is the very essence of reality! It is the most practical way to stay close to the only One who can help us through the challenge.

Be patient, waiting for God's timing.

Expectations can be damaging during a crisis. When we assume that the Lord will solve our problems in a certain way or by a certain time, we set ourselves up for disappointment and frustration.

Someone described patience as accepting a difficult situation without giving God a deadline for removing it. Remember, God's primary purpose in allowing a crisis in the first place is to conform you to Jesus Christ. He is at work in your life and knows exactly how long it will take to produce the results He wants. Ecclesiastes 3:1 says, *"There is an appointed time for everything. And there is a time for every event under heaven."*

The late Larry Burkett used to say with a smile, "God is seldom early, but He's never late." Be patient. Be careful not to set deadlines for the Lord.

Work diligently.

On the morning of September 29, 1982, twelve-year-old Mary Kellerman died after taking a capsule of Extra-Strength Tylenol. Soon after, six other people died, all from the Chicago area. It was discovered that bottles of Tylenol had been tampered with and laced with cyanide. Within 24 hours of the public learning of this tragedy, Tylenol's market share collapsed from 35 percent to 5 percent, and the reputation of its manufacturer, Johnson & Johnson, was seriously threatened.

Johnson & Johnson's CEO, Dr. James E. Burke, a Christian, acted decisively. He assembled a seven-member team of his top managers to focus on the crisis.

Dr. Burke quickly issued a nationwide recall of Tylenol products – an estimated 31 million bottles were in circulation at that time. The company advertised in the media for consumers not to consume any Tylenol products. They also stopped manufacturing and advertising Tylenol.

Johnson & Johnson set up a toll-free 800 number for customers to call if they had questions. Dr. Burke installed a live satellite feed into his office so he could stay on top of the situation, and he regularly made himself available to the media. He communicated truthfully and announced that Tylenol was going to innovate and use safety seal packing – something none of his competitors were using.

When the accountants warned Dr. Burke that these decisions were going to cost more than $150 million, Dr. Burke responded, "Do you remember our company's Credo? Our first responsibility is to our customers. It's worth spending $150 million if it saves lives."

Afterwards, the media gave Johnson & Johnson credit for handling the crisis extraordinarily well. *The Washington Post* wrote, "Johnson & Johnson has effectively demonstrated how a major business ought to handle a disaster." They were applauded for their honesty and the care they exhibited for people.

Customers responded as well. Within a single year, their market share had rebounded and actually increased. Dr. Burke later recalled, "Whenever we cared for the customer in a profound and spiritual way, profits were never a problem."

Glance at the problem, but *gaze* at Christ.

We are to work diligently to solve our problems, but with the recognition that we need the moment-by-moment help and counsel of the Lord who loves us. Think of it this way: we are to *glance* at the problem but *gaze* at Christ. *"Look to the LORD and His strength; seek His face **always**"* (Psalm 105:4, NIV, emphasis added). *". . . let us run with endurance the race that is set before us, fixing our eyes on Jesus, the author and perfecter of faith . . ."* (Hebrews 12:1-2).

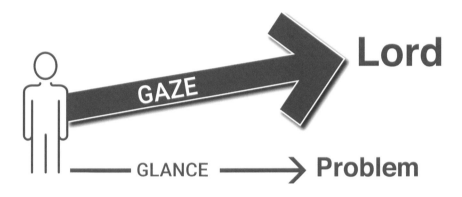

To help you gaze on the Lord, try meditating on Scripture, keeping up a silent conversation with Him through your day, and listening to quality Christian music. One of my friends carries around index cards with favorite Scripture verses in his pocket. If he finds himself in a long line somewhere he uses the time to read and think about God's word.

One of my favorite passages when facing difficulties is Philippians 4:6-7. Every phrase is loaded with meaning. *"Be anxious for **nothing**, but in **every-thing** by prayer and supplication with thanksgiving let your requests be made known to God. And the peace of God, which surpasses all comprehension, will guard your hearts and your minds in Christ Jesus"* (emphasis added).

Forgive others.

Imagine you are a teenager, deeply loved by your father. Your jealous siblings sell you into slavery, and for more than a decade you are a slave and a prisoner. Amazingly, on one unbelievable day, you find yourself elevated to second in command of the world's most powerful nation. Several years later, your starving siblings – the very ones who betrayed you – beg you for food. What's your response: retaliation or forgiveness?

This is the question Joseph had to answer, and his decision was to forgive. How was he able to do this? Because he recognized that God had orchestrated his circumstances – even the ones that were so deeply traumatic and painful. *"God sent me ahead of you . . ."* he told his brothers, *"to save your lives by a great deliverance. So then, it was not you who sent me here, but God"* (Genesis 45:7-8, NIV).

God realizes how critical it is for us to forgive those who have caused or contributed to our crisis, regardless of their motivation. One of the most impressive characteristics of Jesus Christ was His willingness to forgive. Imagine hanging on a cross in unspeakable agony and at the same time praying for those who had crucified you: *"Father, forgive them; for they do not know what they are doing"* (Luke 23:34).

When the apostle Peter asked Jesus if he should forgive someone seven times, Christ responded, *"not seven times, but seventy-seven times"* (Matthew 18:22, NIV). He then told a parable about a servant who was forgiven a large debt by his master, but refused to forgive a fellow servant a small debt. Christ describes what happens to the unforgiving servant: *"In anger his master turned him over to the jailers to be tortured, until he should pay back all he owed. This is how my heavenly Father will treat each of you unless you forgive your brother from your heart"* (Matthew 18:34-35, NIV).

In order to grow more like Christ and experience the benefits He intends for us during a crisis, we must forgive. And more than forgive, we are to be kind, compassionate, and seek to be a blessing. *"Be kind and compassionate to one another, forgiving each other, just as in Christ God forgave you* (Ephesians 4:32, NIV). *"Not returning evil for evil or insult for insult, but giving a blessing instead; for you were called for the very purpose that you might inherit a blessing"* (1 Peter 3:9).

Unforgiveness can be a daily battle, particularly if the crisis has been deeply hurtful. Even so, the person who is harmed most by unforgiveness is the person who refuses to forgive. My wife, Bev, described it as swallowing poison and hoping the other person will die. When we refuse to forgive, the bitterness in our heart can turn toxic, consuming our thoughts and eating away our emotional health. Forgiveness and seeking to bless the other person – as difficult as that seems to contemplate – lead to freedom.

It is imperative to pray regularly for the Lord to give us the *desire* to forgive--and then to give us His love for the people who may have harmed us. Jesus tells us also to pray for them: *"Love your enemies and pray for those who persecute you, so that you may be sons of your Father in heaven"* (Matthew 5:44). It's hard to remain bitter toward someone you are praying for every day.

PERSONAL REFLECTIONS

On a scale of 1 to 10 (with 10 being the best) how well prepared are you for a crisis? Summarize your preparation for your life, family, business (if you have one), and finances.

- Life

- Family

- Business

- Finances

9

ETERNITY
– PART ONE

On Monday, October 25, 1999, the news reported an unfolding story. Air Force jets following a Learjet from Orlando, Florida, were unable to communicate with its pilots. I learned later that two of my close friends and accomplished businessmen, Robert Fraley and Van Ardan, were on that Learjet as it carried them and professional golfer Payne Stewart to their deaths.

One of the most crucial perspectives for us to embrace when handling money is the reality of eternity. Robert and Van, both in their mid-forties, lived with an eternal perspective. Robert had framed these words of Saint Augustine in his workout area: "Take care of your body as though you will live forever; take care of your soul as though you will die tomorrow."

In the New Testament, many of the verses addressed specifically to the wealthy deal with eternity. It is relatively easy for those who live in abject poverty, for those who are physically persecuted, or for those who experience severe chronic pain to look forward to heaven. But what about those with wealth? When you can easily afford and enjoy the best this life offers, it's not easy to consider leaving the good life on earth.

The Lord reveals in the Scriptures that there is a heaven and hell, that there is a coming judgment, and that He will grant eternal rewards unequally. God does this because He loves us. The Lord wants the best for us and wants to motivate us to invest our lives in such a way that we can enjoy an intimate relationship with Him now—and the greatest possible rewards and responsibilities in heaven.

Our failure to view this present life through the lens of eternity robs us of the ability to see our lifespan and our assets in their true light. Scripture urges us again and again to let the reality of our eternal future determine and shape our present life – and the use of our money and possessions.

People who don't know the Lord look at life as a brief period that begins at birth and ends at death. Looking to the future, they see no further than their own life span. With no eternal perspective, they think, *If this life is all there is, why deny myself anything?*

Those who know Christ have an entirely different perspective. We know very well that this life on earth is brief. It's the preface, not the book. It's the trailer, not the movie. As the apostle James put it: "*The length of your lives is as uncertain as the morning fog—now you see it; soon it is gone*" (James 4:14, TLB). Yet this brief period will determine much of our experience in heaven throughout all eternity.

Financial planners try to persuade clients to look down the road instead of simply focusing on today. "Don't think in terms of this year," they will tell you. "Think and plan for 30 years from now." The wise person does indeed think ahead, but far more than 30 years ahead – more like *30 million* years ahead. Someone once said, "He who provides for this life but takes no care for eternity is wise for a moment, but a fool forever." Jesus said it this way: "*What does it profit a man to gain the whole world, and forfeit his soul?*" (Mark 8:36).[5]

Life on earth is short.

The Bible frequently reminds us that life on earth is brief: "[God] *is mindful that we are but dust*" (Psalm 103:14). Our earthly bodies are called "*tents*" (2 Peter 1:13, NIV), temporary dwelling places of our eternal souls. David recognized this and sought to gain God's perspective on the brevity of life.

He asked of the Lord, *"Show me, O L*ORD*, my life's end and the number of my days; let me know how fleeting is my life . . . Each man's life is but a breath. Man is a mere phantom as he goes to and fro: He bustles about, but only in vain; he heaps up wealth, not knowing who will get it"* (Psalm 39:4-6, NIV).

It's especially important for the wealthy to recognize that life on earth is short. The apostle James wasn't shy about telling it straight: *"But the rich person is to glory in his humiliation, because like flowering grass he will pass away. For the sun rises with its scorching heat and withers the grass; and its flower falls off and the beauty of its appearance is destroyed; so also the rich person, in the midst of his pursuits, will fade away"* (James 1:10-11).

Moses realized that true wisdom requires an awareness and understanding of the brevity of our lives. With that in mind, he asked the Lord to help him number the days he had on earth. *"As for the days of our life, they contain seventy years, or if due to strength, eighty years . . . for soon it is gone and we fly away. So teach us to number our days, that we may present to You a heart of wisdom"* (Psalm 90:10, 12).

The greatest surprise of my life is the brevity of life."
– Billy Graham

I encourage you to actually estimate the number of days you have left on earth. If I live as long as an average of my mother and father, I currently have about 1,900 days left. This has helped me focus on investing my life and resources in eternally important matters. In light of the brevity of life, Matthew Henry said, "It ought to be the business of every day to prepare for our last day."

Eternity is long.

Eternity, on the other hand, *never ends*. It is forever. Admittedly, finite minds like ours can't really wrap around a concept like that. But here's an illustration to help us try: Imagine a cable running through the room where you are now. To your right, the cable runs billions of light years, all the way to the end of the universe; to your left, it runs to the other end of the universe. Now imagine that the cable to your left represents eternity past, and the cable to your right, eternity future. Imagine taking out a red marker and making a tiny line on the cable in front of you. That tiny red dash represents your brief life on earth.

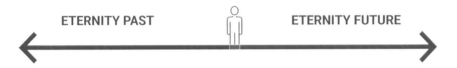

ETERNITY PAST   ETERNITY FUTURE

Most people, however, lacking such an eternal perspective, live their lives as if the mark was everything! They make *mark* choices, live in *mark* houses, drive *mark* cars, wear *mark* clothes, raise *mark* children, and dream *mark* dreams. Devotional writer A. W. Tozer referred to eternity as "the long tomorrow." This is the backdrop against which all the questions of life and the use of our resources must be answered.

ALIENS AND PILGRIMS

Scripture tells us several things about our identity and role on earth. First, *"Our citizenship is in heaven"* (Philippians 3:20), not on earth. Second, *"We are ambassadors for Christ"* (2 Corinthians 5:20), representing Him on earth. Imagine yourself as an ambassador working in a country that is generally hostile toward your own. Naturally, you will want to learn about this new place, see the sights, and become familiar with the people and culture. But suppose you eventually become so assimilated into this foreign country that you begin to regard it as your true home. Your allegiance wavers, and you gradually compromise your position as an ambassador, becoming increasingly ineffective in representing the best interests of your own country.

We must never become too much at home in this world, or we will become ineffective in serving the cause of the kingdom we are here to represent. We are aliens, strangers, and pilgrims on earth. Peter wrote, *"Live out your time as foreigners here in reverent fear"* (1 Peter 1:17, NIV). Another Bible translation uses the words *"strangers and pilgrims"* (1 Peter 2:11, KJV).

Pilgrims are travelers – not settlers – aware that the excessive accumulation of things can distract them and bog them down. Yes, material things are valuable to pilgrims, *but only as they facilitate their mission*. If we aren't careful, our possessions can begin to entrench us in the present world, acting as chains around our legs that keep us from moving in response to God. When our eyes are too focused on the visible, they will be drawn away from the invisible. *"So we fix our eyes not on what is seen, but on what is unseen, since what is seen is temporary, but what is unseen is eternal"* (2 Corinthians 4:18, NIV).

Pilgrims of faith look to the next world. They see their earthly possessions for what they are: useful for kingdom purposes but far too flimsy to trust. Thomas à Kempis, author of *The Imitation of Christ*, said it this way: "Let temporal things serve your use, but the eternal be the object of your desire." [5]

Prosperity knits a man to the World. He feels that he is 'finding his place in it,' while really it is finding its place in him. His increasing reputation, his widening circle of acquaintances, his sense of importance . . . builds up in him a sense of being really at home on earth." – C. S. Lewis, *The Screwtape Letters*

There are two truths that will help us gain a proper perspective of our possessions.

We leave it all behind.

After John D. Rockefeller died, it was reported that his accountant was asked how much he left. The accountant responded, "He left it all." Job said it this way, *"Naked I came from my mother's womb, and naked I shall return there"* (Job 1:21). Paul wrote, *"For we have brought nothing into the world, so we cannot take anything out of it either"* (1 Timothy 6:7).

An English aristocrat proudly spent an entire day showing John Wesley his large estate. At the end of the day the man asked Wesley, "What do you think of my magnificent lands and buildings?" Wesley replied, "I think it will be very hard for you to leave this when you die." [5]

The psalmist observed, *"Do not be afraid when a man becomes rich, when the glory of his house is increased; for when he dies he will carry nothing away; his glory will not descend after him. Though while he lives he congratulates himself – and though men praise you when you do well for yourself – he shall go to the generation of his fathers"* (Psalm 49:16-19).

Everything will be destroyed.

Earthly goods are destined to molder into dust—or disappear in a flash. *"The day of the Lord will come like a thief. The heavens will disappear with a roar; the elements will be destroyed by fire, and the earth and everything in it will be laid bare. Since everything will be destroyed in this way, what kind of people ought you to be? You ought to live holy and godly lives"* (2 Peter 3:10-11, NIV). This eternal perspective of earthly things should motivate us handle them in a way that pleases the Lord.

✎ PERSONAL REFLECTIONS

View the Francis Chan Rope Illustration video (5:59) at ChartingYourLegacy.org, or by using this QR code.

- Take some time to consider and respond. In light of eternity, I will change how I spend my time and money these ways:

- As you reflect on eternity from God's perspective, what three things do you want to accomplish during the rest of your life?

RECOMMENDED RESOURCES

Author Randy Alcorn graciously contributed some of the content and original concepts for this chapter and the next from his book *Money, Possessions, and Eternity*. (Wheaton, IL: Tyndale Publishers, 1989, 2003.) This book is outstanding and we highly recommend it! Visit his web site www.epm.org for a host of excellent materials.

10

ETERNITY – PART TWO

It's uncomfortable to think about judgment. However, because our Lord loves us so deeply, He wants us to realize what will happen in the future. For this reason, God revealed to us that we all will be judged according to our deeds:

- *"He has fixed a day in which He will judge the world in righteousness"* (Acts 17:31).

- *"They will have to give account to him who is ready to judge the living and the dead"* (1 Peter 4:5, NIV).

- *"Nothing in all creation is hidden from God's sight. Everything is uncovered and laid bare before the eyes of him to whom we must give account"* (Hebrews 4:13, NIV).

- *"Everyone will have to give account on the day of judgment for every empty word they have spoken"* (Matthew 12:36, NIV).

- *"God will bring every deed into judgment, including every hidden thing, whether it is good or evil"* (Ecclesiastes 12:14, NIV).

The Bible teaches that all those who do not know Christ will be judged and sent to an unspeakably dreadful destiny. *"I saw a great white throne and him who was seated on it. . . . And I saw the dead, great and small, standing before the throne . . . Each person was judged according to what they had done. . . . Anyone whose name was not found written in the book of life was thrown into the lake of fire"* (Revelation 20:11-15, NIV).

YOU CAN KNOW GOD

Realizing that we can know God personally changes everything. I was twenty-eight years old when I started meeting with several young businessmen. It wasn't long before I was impressed by their business savvy. But more than that, I was attracted to the quality of their lives. I didn't know what they had, but whatever it was, I wanted it.

These men spoke openly of their faith in God. I had grown up going to church, but the religion I had seen modeled during those years meant nothing to me as an adult. I had concluded it was only a fairy tale until a friend described how I could enter into a *personal* relationship with Jesus Christ. He explained several truths from the Bible I had never understood before.

God knows you personally.

The following passages are but a small sample of how personally the Lord is involved in your life:

- **God wrote every day of your life in His book before you were born.** *"Your eyes saw my unformed body; all the days ordained for me were written in your book before one of them came to be. How precious to me are your thoughts, God! How vast is the sum of them! Were I to count them, they would outnumber the grains of sand . . ."* (Psalm 139:16-18, NIV).

- **God made you in your mother's womb**. *"For you created my inmost being; you knit me together in my mother's womb. I praise you because I am fearfully and wonderfully made"* (Psalm 139:13-14, NIV).

- **God is constantly with you**. *"You have searched me, Lord, and you know me. You know when I sit and when I rise; you perceive my thoughts from afar. You discern my going out and my lying down; you are familiar with all my ways. Before a word is on my tongue you, Lord, know it completely"* (Psalm 139: 1-4, NIV).

- **God will personally wipe away every one of your tears in heaven.** *"God's dwelling place is now among the people, and he will dwell with them . . . God himself will be with them and be their God. He will wipe every tear from their eyes . . ."* (Revelation 21:3-4, NIV).

God wants you to know Him personally.

God desires a close relationship with each of us.

- *"For God so loved the world, that He gave His only begotten Son, that whoever believes in Him shall not perish, but have eternal life"* (John 3:16).

- *"I [Jesus] came that they may have life, and have it abundantly"* (John 10:10).

- *"For you know the grace of our Lord Jesus Christ, that though He was rich, yet for your sake He become poor, so that you through His poverty might become rich"* (2 Corinthians 8:9).

Author Richard Foster said, "To think rightly about God is, in an important sense, to have everything right. To think wrongly about God is, in an important sense, to have everything wrong." For this reason, it is crucial for you to recognize how extravagantly God loves you.

Perhaps this example will help you understand the depth of His love. In the 1992 Olympics in Barcelona, Spain, Great Britain had a runner named Derek Redmond who had dreamed all his life of winning the gold medal in the 400-meter race. As the gun sounded for the semifinals, Derek knew he was running the race of his life. Then tragically, as he entered the backstretch, Redmond felt pain shoot up the back of his right leg. A torn hamstring sent him sprawling face down on the track.

Instinctively, Derek struggled to his feet in excruciating pain and began hopping on one leg toward the finish line. Suddenly a large man came bounding from the stands. Flinging aside security guards, he made his way onto the field and threw his arms around Derek. It was Jim Redmond, Derek's father. "Son, you don't have to do this," he said.

"Yes, Dad, I do," Derek assured him.

"All right then, let's finish this together," said the older man. And that's exactly what they did. With the son's head frequently buried in the father's shoulder, they made it to the end of the race as the crowd rose to its feet, weeping and cheering![6]

Derek Redmond did not win the gold medal in the Olympics. But he won something far more valuable. He walked away from the race with the memory of a father who was not only in the stands cheering, but who loved him too much to watch him suffer from a distance – a father who came down out of the stands and entered the race with him, staying beside him every step of the way.

We have a heavenly Father who watches us with eyes of love and affection. He is our Father-God who cared for us too deeply to stay in heaven, looking down on us, watching us fall and fail. Instead, He came down out of the stands and into our race in the person of His precious Son, Jesus Christ. And He is committed to staying in this race with us until we have safely crossed the finish line.[7]

Unfortunately, we are separated from God.

God is holy, which simply means He is perfect, and can't have a relationship with anyone who is not perfect. My friend asked if I had ever sinned – done anything that would disqualify me from perfection. "Many times," I admitted. He explained that every person has sinned, and the consequence of sin is separation from God. *"All have sinned and fall short of the glory of God"* (Romans 3:23). *"Your sins have cut you off from God"* (Isaiah 59:2, TLB).

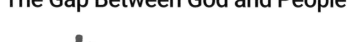

The Gap Between God and People

People (SINFUL)

God (HOLY)

God's only provision to bridge this gap is Jesus Christ.

Jesus Christ died on the cross to pay the penalty for our sin, bridging the gap between God and us.

- Jesus said, *"I am the way, and the truth, and the life; no one comes to the Father but through Me"* (John 14:6).

- *"God demonstrates His own love toward us, in that while we were yet sinners, Christ died for us"* (Romans 5:8).

This personal relationship is a gift from God.

My friend explained that by faith I could receive the free gift of a personal relationship with God. The transaction appeared inequitable. I had learned in business that a transaction happens only when both sides are convinced they are getting more than they are giving up. But now I was being offered a relationship with God, and it was free! *"It is by grace you have been saved, through faith – and this is not from yourselves, it is the gift of God – not by works, so that no one can boast"* (Ephesians 2:8-9, NIV).

The Union Between God and People

I had only to ask Jesus Christ to come into my life to be my Savior and Lord. So I did! As my friends will tell you, I'm a very practical person; if something doesn't work, I stop doing it. I can tell you from more than fifty years of experience that a relationship with God is real. And it is available to you through Jesus Christ. Nothing in life compares with knowing Christ personally. We can experience true peace, joy, and hope when we know Him. It's the only way you can enjoy a truly meaningful life and leave an eternally significant legacy.

If you want to know God and are not certain whether you have this relationship, I encourage you to receive Jesus Christ right now. Pray a prayer similar to the one I prayed: "God, I need you. I'm sorry for my sin. I invite Jesus to come into my life as my Savior and Lord, and to make me the person you want me to be. Thank You for forgiving my sins and giving me the gift of eternal life."

You might have amassed tremendous wealth, but without a relationship with Christ, it won't have any lasting value. If you asked Christ into your life, you have made the most important decision anyone could ever make. *"God has given us eternal life, and this life is in his Son. Whoever has the Son has life; whoever does not have the Son of God does not have life. I [John] write these things to you who believe in the name of the Son of God so that you may know that you have eternal life"* (1 John 5:11-13, NIV).

I urge you to find a church that teaches the Bible, one where you can begin to learn what it means to follow Jesus Christ.

All your life you have been on a treasure hunt. You've been searching for a perfect person and perfect place. Jesus is that person and heaven is that place." – Randy Alcorn

Judgment of believers

After they die, those who know Christ will spend eternity with the Lord in heaven, an unimaginably wonderful place. What we seldom consider, however, is that the entry point to heaven is a judgment.

Scripture teaches that all believers in Christ will give an account of their lives to the Lord. *"We will all stand before the judgment seat of God. So then each one of us will give an account of himself to God"* (Romans 14:10, 12). The result of this will be the gain or loss of eternal rewards. In 1 Corinthians

3:13-15, we read, *"Their work will be shown for what it is, because the [Judgment] Day will bring it to light. . . . If what has been built survives, the builder will receive a reward. If it is burned up, the builder will suffer loss"* (NIV). Our works are what we have done with our time, influence, talents, and resources.

God's Word doesn't treat this judgment as just a meaningless formality before we get on to the real business of heaven. Not at all! Scripture presents it as a monumental event in which things of eternal significance are brought to light.[5]

Motivation and rewards

Why should I follow God's guidance on handling money when it's so much fun to do whatever I please with it? After all, I'm a Christian. I know I'm going to heaven anyway. Why not have the best of both worlds – this one *and* the next? Though few of us would be honest enough to use such language, these questions reflect a common attitude.

The prospect of eternal rewards for our obedience is a neglected key to unlocking our motivation. (How long has it been since you heard a sermon or someone teaching on this?) The apostle Paul was certainly motivated by the prospect of eternal rewards. He wrote, *"I have fought the good fight, I have finished the course, I have kept the faith; in the future there is laid up for me the crown of righteousness, which the Lord, the righteous Judge, will award to me on that day"* (2 Timothy 4:7-8). The Lord appeals not only to our compassion, but also to our eternal self-interest. *"Love your enemies, and do good, and lend, expecting nothing in return; and your reward will be great"* (Luke 6:35).

Unequal rewards in heaven

Some think, *I'll be in heaven, and that's all that matters.*

Well, yes and no. It's really not that simple. On the contrary, Paul spoke about the loss of reward as a *terrible* loss, and the receiving of rewards from Christ as a phenomenal gain.

Author Randy Alcorn states that "Not all Christians will have the same rewards in heaven." John Wesley said, "I value all things only by the price they shall gain in eternity." God's kingdom was the reference point for him. He lived as he did, not because he didn't treasure things but because he treasured the *right* things.

We often miss something in missionary martyr Jim Elliot's famous words, "He is no fool who gives what he cannot keep to gain what he cannot lose." We focus on the first part of that quote: Elliot's willingness to sacrifice. And so we should. At the same time, however, we often overlook the second part: Jim Elliot's motivation for gain. What separated him from many Christians wasn't that he didn't want treasure, but that he wanted *real* treasure. Remember, God loves you deeply. Because He wants the best for you throughout eternity, God has revealed that today's financial sacrifices and service for Him will pay off forever.

The greatest reward we can receive is Christ Himself, and to hear His words, *"Well done, good and faithful servant. You were faithful with a few things, I will put you in charge of many things; enter into the joy of your master"* (Matthew 25:21). There are other rewards as well. I am especially motivated by the one to influence others for Christ.[5]

- *"For what is our hope, our joy, or the crown in which we will glory in the presence of our Lord Jesus when he comes? Is it not you?"* (1 Thessalonians 2:19, NIV).

- *"My brothers and sisters, you whom I love and long for, my joy and crown"* (Philippians 4:1, NIV).

Can you imagine the incredible joy of meeting someone in heaven and learning that you had somehow influenced them to be there – throughout eternity – because of your prayers or the investment of your time and money?

God doesn't object to an investment mentality; rather He commands it, *"Lay up for yourselves treasures in heaven"* (Matthew 6:20, KJV). There is, however, a fundamental question we must ask ourselves as we grow older. Am I moving *closer* to the treasures I have laid up in heaven that will last forever, or am I moving *away* from the treasures I have stockpiled on earth that will become dust?

IMPACTING ETERNITY TODAY

Our daily choices determine what will happen in the future. What we do in this life is of eternal importance. We only live on this earth once. *"It is appointed for men to die once and after this comes judgment"* (Hebrews 9:27). Forget the idea of reincarnation; the Bible directly contradicts it. Once our life on earth is over, we will never have another chance to move the hand of God through prayer, to share Christ with a friend who doesn't know the Savior, to give money to further God's kingdom, or to share with the needy.

Alfred Nobel was a Swedish chemist who made his fortune by inventing dynamite and other powerful explosives that were bought by governments to produce weapons. When Alfred Nobel's brother died, one newspaper accidentally printed Alfred's obituary instead. He was described as a man who became rich by enabling people to kill each other on a massive scale. Shaken by this assessment, Nobel resolved to use his fortune to reward accomplishments that benefited humanity, including what we now know as the Nobel Peace Prize.

Let us put ourselves in Nobel's place. Let us read our own obituary, not as written by uninformed people, but as it would be written from heaven's point of view. Then let us use the rest of our lives to edit that obituary into what we really want it to be—while there is still time! [5]

I loved playing Little League baseball as a young boy. We played on a huge field with towering fences in the outfield. Years later, shortly after my father died, I spent the day walking around my old hometown, reflecting on his life. When I visited the baseball field, I was shocked. It was so small! I could actually step over the outfield fences. While standing there, a thought struck me: *Many of those things that seem so large and important to us today shrink to insignificance in just a few years.*

When I am face to face with Christ and look back on my life, I want to see that the things in which I invested my time, creativity, influence, and money are big things to Him. I don't want to squander my life on things that won't matter throughout eternity.

"

What matters the most in the end, matters most now." – Unknown

What are the choices facing you now? How does an eternal perspective influence your decisions? Martin Luther said his calendar consisted of only two days: "today" and "that Day." May we invest all that we are and have today in light of *that* day.

 PERSONAL REFLECTIONS

- How does the reality of judgment and receiving rewards influence your thinking? Are you prepared for it?

- If you are not prepared, what steps do you need to take?

11

GENEROSITY

Whavitehen Chip Ingram served as pastor of his first church, he was invited to breakfast by the most successful businessman in town.

"I'd like to help the needy in our community," he told Chip, "but I'm too busy. I want to deposit $5,000 in an account for you to give to those you meet who are in need. Then, let's get together once a quarter. You tell me the stories of those you helped, and I'll replenish the account."

Chip experienced amazing freedom and joy giving away the businessman's money. After about a year it dawned on him: the reason Chip enjoyed giving it so much was because it wasn't his money! That's when he realized how he should view his own giving. It was never *his* money that he gave away, it was always the *Lord's* money! Recognizing that God is the owner of all you possess is the foundation to giving generously and joyfully.

Few areas of the wealthy Christian's life can be more challenging than that of giving. Consider these common reactions to giving:

- I can't trust anyone to be a real friend because I feel they're just after my money.

- Once I began giving larger sums of money, it became common knowledge, and I was besieged by requests.

- I can't give with confidence because I don't have time to investigate giving opportunities to determine which are truly worthy.

- I've become disillusioned with some of those I have supported. They haven't been faithful or responsible, and it's made me a little callous toward others who ask.

- I feel uncomfortable tithing to my local church because it would represent too large of a percentage of the church budget.

- I have a large net worth, but I still don't know if it's enough to meet my long-term needs and lifestyle. This has made me reluctant to be more generous.

- I struggle to balance my giving with how much I should provide for my children's inheritance.

- I feel guilty that we aren't more generous.

- Sometimes I feel I'm being subtly manipulated by people whose goals may be worthwhile, but whose means of achieving those goals are questionable.

Some of the most important principles to help the wealthy navigate the ocean of choices without boundaries are those concerning generosity. When properly understood and implemented, they are liberating—and will help you arrive at your home in heaven with treasures awaiting you.

First Timothy 6:17-19 reads, *"Instruct those who are rich in this present world . . . to be generous and ready to share, storing up for themselves the treasure of a good foundation for the future, so that they may take hold of that which is life indeed."* In this passage, which is addressed specifically to the wealthy, we are instructed to be generous givers. When we follow this command, the Lord tells us of two specific benefits that will flow our way: (1) eternal treasures that we will enjoy in the future, and (2) the blessing of taking *"hold of that which is life indeed"* during our time on earth. Can you imagine anything on earth more fulfilling than living the life God intended for you before you were born?

"Money doesn't make you happy; it just makes you unhappy in a better part of town." – David Siegel, timeshare king

"I've never met an unhappy generous person." – Todd Harper, Co-founder of Generous Giving

More Bible verses deal with giving than any other financial topic. I hope you will discover that far from being frustrating, the privilege of giving is one of the most exciting opportunities the Lord has graciously extended to us. Daryl Heald serves with a foundation that receives thousands of grant requests each year. He says, "Sometimes it's challenging to maintain God's perspective when constantly being asked for money. Yet it is an incredible privilege to be asked. When you have this mindset, you view requests with a sense of excitement over the prospect of helping to advance God's kingdom rather than an imposition."

We will examine the four elements of giving: attitudes, advantages, amount, and approach.

Attitudes in Giving

God evaluates our giving on the basis of our *attitude*. His attitude in giving is best summed up in John 3:16: *"For God so **loved** the world, that He **gave** His only begotten Son"* (emphasis added). Did you notice the sequence? Because God loved, He gave. He set the example of giving motivated by love.

An attitude of love in giving is simply irreplaceable: *"If I give all my possessions to feed the poor . . . but do not have love, it profits me nothing"* (1 Corinthians 13:3). It is hard to imagine anything more commendable than giving everything to the poor. But if it's done with the wrong attitude – without love – it nets the giver precisely zero. There will be no benefits to him or her whatsoever.

Our basis for giving out of a heart filled with love is the recognition that our gifts, though given for the benefit of people, are actually given to the Lord Himself. An example of this is Numbers 18:24: *"The tithe of the sons of Israel, which they offer as an offering to the Lord, I have given to the Levites for an inheritance."* If giving is merely to a church, ministry, or needy individual, it's only "charity." But if it is to the Lord, it becomes an act of worship. Because God is our Creator, Savior, and faithful Provider, one tangible way we can express our love is by giving our gifts to Him.

We also are to give cheerfully. *"Each one must do just as he has purposed in his heart, not grudgingly or under compulsion, for God loves a cheerful giver"* (2 Corinthians 9:7). The original Greek word for "cheerful" is "Hilarios," which translates into the English word "hilarious." We are to be outrageously joyful givers!

Now, how do we develop this hilarity in our giving? Consider the churches of Macedonia. *"Now, brethren, we wish to make known to you the grace of God which has been given in the churches of Macedonia, that in a great ordeal of affliction their abundance of joy and their deep poverty overflowed in the wealth of their liberality"* (2 Corinthians 8:1-2).

How did the Macedonians, who were in terrible circumstances – *"their great affliction and deep poverty"* – still manage to give with an *"abundance of joy"*? The answer is in verse 5: *"They first gave themselves to the Lord and to us by the will of God."* The key to cheerful giving is to submit ourselves to Christ, asking Him to direct how much He wants us to give. Only then are we in a position to give with the proper attitude and reap any of the advantages.

From God's point of view, the attitude is more important than the amount. Jesus emphasized this in Matthew 23:23: *"Woe to you, scribes and Pharisees, hypocrites! For you tithe mint and dill and cummin, and have neglected the weightier provisions of the law: justice and mercy and faithfulness. . ."* Calculators in hand, the Pharisees had been careful to give the correct amount – down to the last mint leaf in their gardens! But because of their wrong attitude, Christ rebuked them. He looks past the amount of the gift to the *heart* of the giver. For giving to be of any value, it must be done from a heart of love.

Stop and examine yourself. What is your attitude toward giving?

Advantages of Giving

Obviously, a gift benefits the recipient. The local church continues its ministry, the hungry are fed, and missionaries are sent. But in God's economy, the giver benefits more than the receiver. *". . . Remember the words of the Lord Jesus, that He Himself said, 'It is more blessed to give than to receive'"* (Acts 20:35). This is one of the choicest privileges the Lord has extended to those who are wealthy. As we examine the Bible, we find that the giver benefits in four distinct areas.

1. Increase in Intimacy

Above all else, giving directs our attention and heart to Christ. Matthew 6:21 tells us, *"For where your treasure is, there will your heart be also."* Not long ago, I invested in a particular stock for the first time. Although I had never regularly checked its value before acquiring it, I found myself reading reports concerning the company and pulling up the stock on my smart phone daily. Isn't it funny how that works? The more money I invested in the company, the more attention I paid to it.

My heart followed my treasure.

And guess what? It *always* works that way.

This is why it is so necessary to give each gift to the person of Jesus Christ. When you give your gift to Him, your heart will automatically be drawn to the Lord. I have witnessed that very dynamic countless times—not only in my own life, but in the lives of so many others that have habitually given to Christ.

Giving is one of the responsibilities of a steward, and the more faithful you are in your generosity, the more you can *"enter into the joy of your Master"* (Matthew 25:21). Imagine that the following sentence is underlined, bold, and highlighted in neon red. It is *that* important: Nothing in life can compare to experiencing His joy and knowing Christ more intimately.

2. Increase in Character

Our heavenly Father wants us as His children to be conformed to the image of Jesus Christ. The character of Christ is that of an unselfish giver. Unfortunately, humans are by nature selfish. One of the ways we become conformed to Christ is by habitual giving. Someone once said, "Giving is not God's way of raising money; it is God's way of raising people into the likeness of His Son." For us to develop into the people the Lord wants us to be, we must learn how to share our possessions freely.

We are most like God when we are giving." – Author Max Lucado

3. Increase in Heaven

Matthew 6:20 reads, *"But store up for yourselves treasures in heaven, where moth and rust do not destroy, and where thieves do not break in and steal"* (NIV). Jesus didn't tell us we are wrong in wanting to store up treasures. On the contrary, He commanded us to do it. He was simply saying, "Stop storing them in the wrong place, and start storing them in the right place." Christ's primary argument against amassing material wealth wasn't that it was bad in itself, but simply that it was a poor investment. Material things just won't stand the test of time and eternity.

What does it mean to store treasures in heaven instead of on earth? It means that God offers us the incredible opportunity to trade earthly goods and currency for eternal kingdom rewards. By putting our money and possessions in His treasury, we assure ourselves of eternal rewards beyond our comprehension.

Consider the implication of this offer. We can trade temporal possessions that we cannot keep anyway to gain eternal possessions that we cannot lose. Imagine for a moment that you temporarily live in a foreign country whose currency laws allow you to convert its currency into your country's money *only* if you send it along while you live in the foreign country. You can't take it with you when you leave. What will you do with your foreign money?

There is only one smart answer: you would cash in your foreign currency and send it home before leaving the country.

In the same way, the currency of this world will be worthless at our death. You won't be able to take so much as a nickel with you. When you think about it, this knowledge should radically affect our investment strategy. For us to accumulate vast earthly treasures in the face of our inevitable future is equivalent to stockpiling foreign money despite its eventual worthlessness.[5]

The Lord tells us that there really is something akin to the "First National Bank of Heaven." Paul wrote, *"Not that I seek the gift itself, but I seek for the profit which increases to your account"* (Philippians 4:17). There is an account for each of us in heaven that we will be privileged to enjoy for eternity. And while it is true that we "can't take it with us," Scripture teaches that we can make deposits to our heavenly account before we die.

Don't read over this too quickly.

Let this truth sink into the crevices of your mind.

YOU DON'T LOSE WHAT YOU GIVE. In fact, you will be able to enjoy it *forever*. It's the greatest return on investment you could ever imagine.

Kingdom currency is the only medium of exchange recognized by the Son of God, whose government will last forever. The currency of heaven is our present faithful service and use of our resources for Him. The payoff in eternity will be *"the treasure of a good foundation for the future"* (1 Timothy 6:19) consisting of treasures we will be able to enjoy forever.

4. Increase on Earth

Most people look at giving as a pie. When they give away a slice of the pie, they have less of it left for themselves. Scripture, however, paints the concept in a much different light. According to the Bible, we should view generosity more like a farmer planting seeds that will grow, multiply, and yield a crop in the future. Nurture an investor mentality – instead of giving your resources away, you are investing for the future.

Many believe that generosity results only in spiritual blessings, not in a material increase flowing to the giver. Some who hold this view are reacting to those who teach a "giving to get" motive. You may have heard some teach that if you give, God will always massively multiply your gift in financial returns to you.

Let's examine the clear teaching of Scripture. Proverbs 11:24-25 reads, *"There is one who scatters, and yet increases all the more, and there is one who withholds what is justly due, and yet it results only in want. The generous man will be prosperous, and he who waters will himself be watered."*

Examine 2 Corinthians 9:6-11*: "Now this I say, he who sows sparingly will also reap sparingly; and he who sows bountifully will also reap bountifully . . . God is able to make all grace abound to you, so that always having all sufficiency in everything, you may have an abundance for every good deed; as it is written, 'He scattered abroad, He gave to the poor, His righteousness endures forever.' Now He who supplies seed to the sower and bread for food will supply and multiply your seed for sowing and increase the harvest of your righteousness; you will be enriched in everything for all liberality."*

As the Circle of Generosity demonstrates, these verses clearly teach that giving results in a material increase: *". . . will also reap bountifully . . . always having all sufficiency in everything . . . may have an abundance . . . will supply and multiply your seed . . . you will be enriched in everything."*

But note carefully **why** the Lord returns a material increase: *"Always having all sufficiency in everything, you may have an abundance for every good deed . . . will supply and multiply your seed for sowing . . . you will be enriched in everything for all liberality."* The Lord creates an abundance so that we may continue to give – and even increase our giving. This is illustrated in the circle of giving.

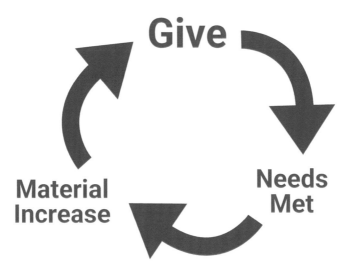

Why, then, does the Lord reveal that our giving will result in material increase? Because He wants us to recognize that He is behind the multiplication of our resources. God has chosen to be invisible, but He wants us to experience His reality. When we give, we should do so with a sense of expectancy – anticipating the Lord to provide a material increase, but not knowing when or how He may choose to provide it. In my experience, He can be very creative!

I have experienced this both in my business and later, after beginning Compass. I have repeatedly seen the Lord entrust significant assets to those who have been generous. Usually, they have had to work hard and wrestle with various business or investment challenges; nevertheless, God has entrusted them with additional resources.

✏️ PERSONAL REFLECTIONS

View the Randy Alcorn – Joy of Giving video (8:07) at ChartingYourLegacy.org, or by using this QR code.

- What in the Joy of Giving video most impacted your thinking?

- Describe the challenges and experiences that have shaped your attitudes toward generosity.

- After prayerfully evaluating your attitude toward generosity, how would you describe it? Do you need to change your attitude toward giving? If so, in what way?

AMOUNT AND APPROACH TO GIVING

When deciding to give, the proper perspective is important. Too many view giving as a joyless obligation, in part, because the Lord commands us to give. However, when it comes to generosity, God wants something *for* us, not *from* us. His objective is that giving would become a delight not a duty.

The foundation of the tithe (giving ten percent).

Let's survey what the Scripture says about how much to give. In the Old Testament, the tithe (ten percent) was required. The Lord condemns the children of Israel in Malachi 3:8-9 for not tithing properly: *"Will a man rob God? Yet you are robbing Me! But you say, 'How have we robbed Thee?' In tithes and offerings. You are cursed with a curse, for you are robbing Me!"*

In addition to the tithe, there were various offerings. Beyond these, the Lord made special provisions to provide for the needs of the poor: every seven years all debts were forgiven, every fifty years the land was returned to the original land-owning families, and there were special rules for harvesting that allowed the poor to glean behind the harvesters and along the edges of the fields. Ruth is an example of a needy person who gleaned in the field of Boaz.

What I like about the tithe is that it is systematic and easy to compute.

The *danger* of the tithe is the view that once I have given it, I move on feeling satisfied and say, "Well, I'm done and have fulfilled all my obligations to give." And that is not the spirit of Biblical giving. For the wealthy, the tithe should be the beginning, not the limit of their generosity.

In the New Testament, the emphasis is giving in proportion to the material resources one has received – *"Each of you put aside and save* [for giving], *as he may prosper"* (1 Corinthians 16:2). *"And in the proportion that any of the disciples had means, each of them determined to send a contribution"* (Acts 11:29).

Take note how Jesus paid special attention to sacrificial giving. *"He sat down opposite the treasury, and began observing how the multitude were putting money into the treasury; and many rich people were putting in large sums. And a poor widow came and put in two small copper coins, which amount to a cent. And calling His disciples to Him, He said to them, 'Truly I say to you, this poor widow put in more than all the contributors to the treasury; for they all put in out of their surplus, but she, out of her poverty, put in all she owned, all she had to live on'"* (Mark 12:41-44).

Take a minute or two to think about this familiar passage.

- From God's point of view, the one with the least gave the most.

- The rich were generous, but the poor widow was commended by Christ Himself because she sacrificially gave *all* she had.

- She was giving by faith, trusting that the Lord would provide her needs.

The Lord isn't saying here that all of us must give all that we have. But it's clear that He commended and drew attention to this woman's sacrificial gift. How can those of us who are wealthy give in a way that requires sacrifice and faith? Consider this point: she gave from her net worth, while I have a hunch that the rich were only giving from their income.

How will the Lord ask you to be generous in the coming days? I couldn't begin to answer that question. I can only encourage you to seek His direction as you consider going beyond a modest fixed percentage of your income.

How much should we give? To answer this question, I suggest several steps:

- **Remember the Lord is the owner of all you have.** He has chosen to place you as steward over much, and has extended to you the privilege and responsibility of handling money His way. There is a difference between philanthropy and biblical stewardship. We must all answers the questions, *Who owns it? Whom am I serving? And whom am I trying to please?* But the steward will answer these questions quite differently from the philanthropist. For the steward, God is the answer to all three.

  When King David prayed during the celebration of the generous offering for the building of God's temple, he said, *"But who am I, and who are my people, that we should be able to give as generously as this? Everything comes from you, and we have given you only what comes from your hand"* (1 Chronicles 29:14, NIV). This is stunning! God first gives to us so that we in turn can give to Him to fulfill His eternal purposes on earth.

- **Submit yourself to Him.** This is the single most important step. Remember what we learned about the Macedonians who were poor and yet managed to give with joy. The secret to their giving was that *"They first gave themselves to the Lord"* (2 Corinthians 8:5). It is crucial that you submit yourself to Christ, asking for Him to direct how much He wants you to give. Take time and get away from your normal activity and busyness to pray. Ask for His direction and a willingness to obey Him.

- **Answer the question:** Why did God give me my resources?

- **Evaluate your giving habits.** Have you established an artificial barrier for your generosity? I know of some that won't write a check for more than $10,000, even if they feel passionately about a ministry or a need.

- **Where do you want your heart to go?** Please answer this question in the light of what Jesus said, *"For where your treasure is, there will your heart be also"* (Matthew 6:21). Based on this passage, here's an observation that some will consider radical: If we want our hearts to be drawn toward Jesus Christ, we need to be giving more to Him than we are saving and investing. Our savings and investments are competing with Christ for our affections and trust.

Just as the earth has more gravitational pull than the moon because it has a greater mass, my heart will be drawn to either my savings and investments or to the Lord. It all depends upon where I place more of my treasure.

APPROACH TO GIVING

Several additional principles are helpful to understand.

Giving should be a priority.

"Honor the LORD from your wealth, and from the first of all your increase" (Proverbs 3:9). As soon as we receive any income, we should set aside the amount we are going to give. This habit helps us remember to put Christ first in all we do – and defeats the temptation to spend the portion we have decided to give.

Giving should be without presumption.

Roger Smith founded an insurance company and invested twenty-five years of his life growing it into a national market leader. A half-dozen companies wanted to acquire his company. He finally decided to merge with a Fortune 500 corporation whose stock Roger felt was undervalued and would soon dramatically increase. For the first time in his life, Roger controlled significant liquid assets. He decided not to give to the Lord's work at the time of the merger, reasoning that he would be able to give even more after the stock increased in value. Instead, it lost tens of millions in value during the two years following the merger.

Many postpone giving, assuming that "an even better time is coming" as the business grows or the investments perform well. By doing so, however, they have violated the principle of presuming upon tomorrow. James 4:13-15 warns us, *"Come now, you who say, 'Today or tomorrow, we shall go to such and such a city, and spend a year there and engage in business and make a profit.' Yet you do not know what your life will be like tomorrow. You are just a vapor that appears for a little while and then vanishes away. Instead, you ought to say, 'If the Lord wills, we shall live and also do this or that.'"*

If you can give now, give. Don't wait.

A growing number of people are using donor advised funds, such as the National Christian Foundation, to give funds, stocks, or businesses even before deciding who the ultimate recipient will be.

Giving should be without pride.

Matthew 6:1-4 reads, *"Beware of practicing your righteousness before men to be noticed by them; otherwise you have no reward with your Father who is in heaven. When therefore you give alms, do not sound a trumpet before you, as the hypocrites do in the synagogues and in the streets, that they may be honored by men. Truly I say to you, they have their reward in full. But when you give alms, do not let your left hand know what your right hand is doing that your alms may be in secret; and your Father who sees in secret will repay you."*

Don't you love the Lord's word picture here? Your right hand is writing checks while your left hand is oblivious to the whole operation. Now *that* is being discreet. But here is the principle: If you want to experience any of the

Lord's benefits, your giving cannot be motivated out of a desire to attract attention to yourself or impress others.

Major giving is best done after due diligence.

Spontaneous giving should characterize followers of Christ. The best example I know is the late Ward Correll. Every Monday his secretary would cash a check and bring him ten $100 bills. Ward would give them away spontaneously to the needy, pastors, those serving in ministry, or anyone else he sensed the Lord wanted him to encourage. Recipients often wept for joy as they realized God was meeting their financial needs during a time of personal crisis.

Before making major gifts, it's prudent to make sure the gift will be wisely spent for the purpose it was granted. The apostle Paul is an example of carefully administering a significant gift.

> "We are sending along with him [Titus] the brother who is praised by all the churches . . . he was chosen by the churches to accompany us as we carry the offering, which we administer in order to honor the Lord Himself. . . **We want to avoid any criticism of the way we administer this liberal gift. For we are taking pains to do what is right, not only in the eyes of the Lord but also in the eyes of man**" (2 Corinthians 8:18-21, NIV, emphasis added).

Here are some basic questions to ask before granting a major gift:

- Who serves on the Board of Directors and how many are independent? What compensation do they receive from serving on the board?

- How much total compensation does each executive receive?

- Does the organization have any related-party transactions? If so, what are they?

- What percentage of total income is spent on fund raising?

- Do they make public their IRS 990 tax return and an annual audit conducted by an independent CPA?

- What will the gift accomplish, and is there a budget for its use?

- Is the leader of the organization a humble, godly person? Is there a clear strategy to identify the successor?

⬤ PERSONAL REFLECTIONS

- What does it mean to you to "give as one prospers" and how has this principle impacted how much you give?

- Prayerfully (with your spouse if you are married) seek the Lord's guidance to determine how much you sense you should give.

CHAPTER

PLACES FOR GIVING

The New Testament tells us to be careful and attentive to our giving in two primary areas. To whom and in what proportion we give will vary with the needs God's Spirit puts on the heart of each follower of Christ. Place number one:

The local church, Christian workers, and ministries

Throughout its pages, the Bible focuses on maintenance of the ministry. The Old Testament priesthood was to receive specific support: *"And to the sons of Levi, behold, I have given all the tithe in Israel . . . in return for their service which they perform . . ."* (Numbers 18:21). And the New Testament teaching on ministerial support is just as strong. Unfortunately, some have wrongly taught poverty for Christian workers. For this reason, many believe that those who serve in various forms of Christian ministry should be poor. This position is neither wise, just, nor scriptural. *"Pastors who do their work well should be paid well and should be highly appreciated, especially those who work hard at both preaching and teaching"* (1 Timothy 5:17, TLB).

How many Christian workers have been driven to distraction from their ministry by inadequate support? God never intended His servants to exist at the level of bare subsistence. As someone has said, "The poor and starving pastor should exist only among poor and starving people."

People have asked Bev and me if we give only to our church. In our case, the answer is no. We do make it a priority to give to our church, because this is a tangible expression of our commitment to it. But we also give to others who have had an impact on our walk with Christ: *"And let the one who is taught the word share all good things with him who teaches"* (Galatians 6:6).

The Poor

In Matthew 25:34-45 we are confronted with one of the most exciting and yet sobering truths in Scripture. Read this passage carefully: *"Then the King will say . . . 'for I was hungry and you gave Me something to eat; I was thirsty, and you gave Me drink' . . . then the righteous will answer Him, saying, 'Lord, when did we see You hungry, and feed You, or thirsty, and give You drink?' . . . the King will answer and say to them, 'Truly I say to you, to the extent that you did it to one of these brothers of Mine, even the least of them,* **you did it to Me.'** *Then He will also say to those on His left, 'Depart from Me, accursed ones, into the eternal fire . . . for I was hungry, and you gave Me nothing to eat; I was thirsty, and you gave Me nothing to drink . . . to the extent that you did not do it to one of the least of these,* **you did not do it to Me.'"**

In some mysterious way we can't begin to wrap our minds around, Jesus, the Creator of all things, personally identifies Himself with the poor. When we share with the poor, we are actually sharing with Jesus Himself. And if that truth seems staggering, then buckle your seatbelt, because the reciprocal is *terrifying.* When we do not give to the poor, we leave Christ Himself hungry and thirsty. When we neglect those in need, we neglect the Son of God Himself—and He knows it, feels it, and will call us to account for it.

Don't ask me how that could be. I just know that it's a spiritual truth, declared by Jesus shortly before going to the cross.

During Christ's earthly ministry, He gave consistently to the poor. It's especially revealing that during the Last Supper, after Jesus told Judas to go (in order to carry out the betrayal), the writer adds this comment: *"Now no one . . . knew for what purpose He had said this to him. For some were supposing, because Judas had the money box, that Jesus was saying to him, 'Buy things we have need of for the feast'; or else, that he should give something to the poor"* (John 13:28-29).

Giving to the poor was such a natural, consistent part of Jesus' life that the disciples just assumed He was sending Judas either to buy food for their own needs or to give to the poor – no other alternative entered their minds!

It is a small wonder that after Paul meets with the disciples to discuss his calling as a minister to the Gentiles, this statement is made: *"They* [the disciples] *only asked us to remember the poor – the very thing I also was eager to do"* (Galatians 2:10).

It's truly mind-blowing to think of all the theological issues the disciples could have discussed with Paul. But at that time, they only mentioned one: remembering the poor. Now that should tell us something!

Two areas of our Christian life are affected by giving or lack of giving to the poor:

Prayer

A lack of giving to the poor could be a source of unanswered prayer. *"Is this not the fast which I choose . . . divide your bread with the hungry and bring the homeless poor into the house . . . then you will call and the LORD will answer"* (Isaiah 58:6-9*). "He who shuts his ear to the cry of the poor will also cry himself and not be answered"* (Proverbs 21:13). The Lord pays attention to everything we say and do, but He seems to take special note of our attitude and generosity to the poor and disadvantaged among us.

Knowing the Lord intimately

The person who refuses or neglects to care for the poor does not know the Lord intimately. *"He pled the cause of the afflicted and the needy; then it was well. Is not that what it means to know Me, declares the Lord?"* (Jeremiah 22:16).

Giving to the poor has been discouraged in part, because of government programs and give-aways. But that really should have no impact on our responsibility to care for the needy. No matter what the government does or does not choose to do, I believe that it's the responsibility of Christians to meet the needs of the poor. The government often treats the poor impersonally, while Christians have the opportunity to show sensitivity and treat men and women with dignity. We can also develop one-on-one relationships with the poor to meet their immediate physical needs. Then we can focus on their longer-term physical and spiritual needs – lovingly equipping those who are capable of becoming self-supporting.

Job is a wonderful example of proactively seeking to help the needy. *"I delivered the poor who cried for help, and the orphan who had no helper . . . I made the widow's heart sing for joy . . . I was eyes to the blind, and feet to the lame. I was a father to the needy, and* **I investigated the case which I did not know**" (Job 29:12-16, emphasis added).

The most powerful example of this for me was when I visited a very successful businessman, Frank Vincent, and his wife, Kim, at their home. After moving to our community only a month earlier, they had already invited a needy couple to live in their home and were actively involved with several local ministries serving the poor. Frank and Kim literally investigated the case which they did not know.

You can start by asking the Lord to bring one poor person into your life, praying a prayer something like this: "Father God, by Your grace create in me the desire to share with the poor. Bring a poor person into my life so that I might learn what it really means to give." This will be a significant maturing step in your relationship with Christ.

Although this area of giving can be frustrating at times, the potential benefits for the giver make it one of the most exciting and fulfilling areas in our entire Christian life.

Secular charities

Numerous secular charities (such as schools, fraternal orders, or organizations formed to conquer diseases) compete vigorously for our gift dollars. Scripture doesn't specifically address whether or not we should give to these charities. Bev and I decided not to support these organizations with a large percentage of our gifts. Here is our reasoning: While many people from many different backgrounds support secular charities, only those who know the Lord support the ministries of Christ. We give to secular charities when either the solicitor is a friend we want to encourage or influence for Christ, or when we sense the Lord's specific prompting.

Purpose of being entrusted with much

When looking at the accumulation of wealth in human history, we see that the trillions of dollars that exist today were mostly generated in just a few generations. For all of human history until the industrial Revolution of the 1700s, extreme wealth was limited to royalty.

Today, American Christians are the wealthiest community of believers in world history. We believe the Lord has chosen this era for wealth creation to fulfill His purposes." – Authors John Cortines and Greg Bauman

Todd Harper, the Co-founder of Generous Giving, said this:

> *"For years and years, United States oil production continued to slowly decline. People felt that reducing our dependence on foreign oil was impossible. But a few years ago, creative engineers and entrepreneurs discovered hydraulic fracturing, and everything changed. Nationally, production is up 50 percent. Geologists knew the resource was there – they just had not figured out how to get it.*

"We believe giving by followers of Christ is in the same place. We are in the midst of figuring out how to begin releasing our tremendous wealth, which has been locked up within families, and begin mobilizing it to accomplish great works for the glory of God. The giving rate, which has been flat for so long, could start moving up, just as our oil production reversed a decades-old trend."

Pastor Andy Stanley suggests a place to start: "What you want for *everyone*, do for *one*." Will Pope, an Oklahoma oil and gas entrepreneur, and his wife, Renee, had their lives changed on a mission trip to Haiti. Their host exposed them to teenagers who had tremendous potential but couldn't afford the education needed to maximize their abilities. They began by funding high school, college, and leadership training for one exceptionally bright young man. They were so encouraged by the impact of this investment on the young man, that today they fund the education and leadership training of hundreds of teens in developing countries.

What opportunities has God placed on your heart to help fund?

Summary

We've covered a lot of information concerning giving in the last three chapters. Allow me to briefly recap: The Lord has entrusted you with significant assets and asks you to handle them His way. One of the privileges God has extended to you is the opportunity to be generous. Although many view giving as an uncomfortable imposition, from a biblical perspective it is a choice opportunity to invest for eternity.

✎ PERSONAL REFLECTIONS

View the story of Pete and Debbie Ochs – Jail House
Generosity (8:23) at ChartingYourLegacy.org, or by using
this QR code.

- What was the most inspirational part of the Pete and Debbie
  Ochs story to you?

- List the top three organizations that receive your giving.

- How does Jesus Christ identify with the poor?

- Are you currently giving to the poor? If not, what is hindering you?

14

FAMILY – EQUIPPING CHILDREN

Every family has a history. Flip through a photo album to the early years when time is measured by births, missing baby teeth, and first days at school. Turn the page to a season of carpools and sports. It's light speed from then on out! Dating, diplomas, and weddings come front and center. But by the time most parents are framing the grandkids' pictures, they have learned to savor their own family's history, to appreciate what has passed.

Wrapped up in every family history – threaded invisibly throughout the memories – is money. That's right, money. How a family gets, grapples with, guards, and gives money is all part of who that family is. Money, in part, defines a family. And just as great memories like special events or vacations don't happen by accident, a family's view of money doesn't simply materialize out of thin air.

Photo albums don't create family history or values; they chronicle them. They capture something as it happens and preserve it for others to be reminded of later.

But in order to store a memory, you first have to *make* it.

It is the role of the parent to determine the culture of a family, to decide what is worth doing, worth believing, and worth letting go. And then, if a mom and dad plan to instill certain values into their children – planting them so deeply that their children will instill them in *their* children – they have to be very intentional.[8]

Many affluent people have maintained healthy relationships with their immediate and extended families. They also have trained their children to handle money wisely. However, as we have learned earlier, wealth brings with it a unique set of challenges. For the affluent, raising godly children and grandchildren is far more complex than for people with average means. Clashing attitudes about wealth, saving, and spending can make it exceedingly difficult to nurture close relationships with spouses, siblings, and in-laws.

David Johnson's banking empire was crumbling. He was forced to begin selling assets to meet obligations. One evening he announced to his wife and two young sons that he had sold one of their five personal airplanes – the jet. James, his seven-year-old son, began weeping. When asked why he was crying, James wailed, "Dad, it was our *only* jet!" Only then did David understand the impact that his free-spending lifestyle had on his children.

Parents and teachers spend years preparing youth for occupations but generally less than a few hours teaching them the value and use of the money they will manage during their lifetimes. Learning to handle money is a crucial part of a child's education, a part for which the parents must take primary responsibility. Proverbs 22:6 reads, *"Train up a child in the way he should go, even when he is old he will not depart from it."*

Many men can make a fortune but very few can build a family."
– J. S. Bryan

Overall Strategy

The fundamental strategy for training children to handle money is the *Little-Big* principle found in Luke 16:10: *"He who is faithful in a very little thing is faithful also in much."* As children prove faithful with small responsibilities, they are prepared to assume greater ones. After they handle quarters wisely, they are ready for a few dollars. When they manage a few dollars well, they are prepared for more responsibility.

Parents should be as systematic in equipping children to handle money as teachers are in teaching them to write. Children first learn the alphabet, and then how to spell "cat." Each year they learn more complex words and grammar. Finally, they are able to write sophisticated term papers.

The goal is to steadily increase responsibility so that children are independently managing all their finances (with the exception of food and shelter) by their senior year in high school. This way, parents are available to advise their children as they make financial decisions while still at home.

Regardless of how much children will receive in the future through trust funds, gifting, business ownership, or inheritance, it is essential that they be trained to live within spending boundaries. Too many teens from affluent families have unlimited access to money or credit cards – a fact that completely defeats the effectiveness of the *Little-Big* strategy.

Parents should become *MVP Parents*. MVP is an acrostic that describes the three methods to teach children God's way of handling money:

- **Modeling**
- **Verbal communication**
- **Practical experiences**

Modeling

Never doubt it: children absorb parental attitudes toward money like a thirsty sponge soaks up water. Parents must model how to handle money God's way. Paul recognized the importance of example when he said, *"Be imitators of me, just as I also am of Christ"* (1 Corinthians 11:1).

Luke 6:40 tells us, *". . . Everyone, after he has been fully trained, will be like his teacher."* Another way of saying this is that we reproduce what we are. Affluent parents must carefully examine what they are communicating to their children concerning their values. The message can be confusing when lifestyles directly contradict verbal instruction.

Verbal Communication

We must verbally instruct our children in the ways of the Lord as we go about our daily routine. The Lord charged the Israelites, *"These words, which I am commanding you today, shall be on your heart. You shall teach them diligently to your sons* [and daughters] *and shall talk of them when you sit in your house and when you walk by the way and when you lie down and when you rise up"* (Deuteronomy 6:6-7). In other words, consistently tell your children how practical biblical truths apply to everyday life, including handling money.

Practical Experiences

Give your children opportunities to apply what they have heard and seen. Design experiences that are appropriate for their age and unique personality. Young children, for example, are not yet able to grasp abstract concepts, so their practical experiences need to be tangible and easy to understand. This is especially important as our financial system becomes more electronic with credit and debit cards, Internet banking, and Internet equity accounts and trading.

We all learn the most through practical experiences. According to studies, we absorb only 10 percent through formal teaching, 20 percent by entering into a coaching relationship, but 70 percent from experience and challenging assignments. What's the bottom line here? Invest time in designing practical experiences for the younger generation. You can visit ChartingYourLegacy. org for some suggestions.

Learning Money Management

As soon as children are ready for school, they should begin to receive an income to manage. Parents need to decide whether the income must be earned or given as an allowance.

If you choose to give an allowance, assign the children routine chores, without pay, as their share of the family work. If the chores aren't done, the child shouldn't receive the allowance.

The amount of the income will vary according to the child's age and ability to earn. At first, of course, this will be a new experience and the child will make many mistakes. Don't hesitate to let the "law of natural consequences" run its course. You will be tempted to help little Johnny when he spends all of his income the first day on an unwise purchase. Neither he nor you will like his having to live the rest of the week without other things he wants or maybe even needs. *But don't bail him out!* His mistakes will be his best teacher.

Parents should establish boundaries and offer advice on how to spend money, but children must have freedom of choice within those boundaries. Excessive restrictions will only reduce opportunities to learn. The first few quarters will make a lasting impression.

Every Saturday morning, I used to bicycle to the corner store with my young son, Matthew, to buy him a pack of his favorite gum. Despite my advice, he would consume the entire pack that first day. When he started to receive income, we decided that Matthew should buy his own gum. I will never forget the pained expression on his face as he came out of the store with his first purchase. "Daddy, this gum cost me all my money!" he blurted. For the first time, he rationed it with tender care, and that pack of gum lasted more than a week.

As children grow in their ability and demonstrate wise spending patterns, parents should increase their income.

Budgeting

When children start to receive an income, teach them to budget. Begin with a simple system consisting of a three-jar bank, each jar labeled separately: "Give," "Save," and "Spend." Children distribute a portion of their income into each jar. This establishes a basic budget using visual control. Even a six-year-old can understand that when the jar is empty, there is no more money to spend!

As children grow and become responsible for additional spending categories, such as school clothes and recreation, transition them to the envelope system of budgeting. They distribute their income among several labeled envelopes; when an envelope is empty, they have no more to spend for that purpose.

Parents of teens should require an accounting of the previous week's income before giving additional income. Training them to use a budgeting software program or an online budget is essential—and worth every bit of effort you invest into it.

Teaching children to become wise consumers is yet another essential facet of budget training. They need to learn shopping skills and to become aware of the powerful influence of advertising and the danger of impulse spending.

Saving and Investing

The habit of saving should be established as soon as children receive an income. Open a savings account in the child's name. As children mature, expose them to various types of investments such as stocks, bonds, and real estate. Teach them the benefits of compounding.

Children should have both short-term and long-term saving programs. The younger the child, the more important it is to set some short-term achievable goals. To four-year-olds, a week seems like a lifetime to save for a small purchase. They won't understand saving for their future education, but will get excited about saving for a toy.

Debt

It is also important to teach the cost of money and debt. Roger Getty loaned his daughter and son the money to buy bicycles. He drew up a credit agreement with a repayment schedule that included the interest charged. After the children completed the long process of paying off the loan, the family celebrated with a "mortgage burning" ceremony. Roger said his children appreciated those bikes more than any of their other possessions, and they vowed to avoid debt in the future.

Giving

The best time to establish the habit of giving is when children are young. Some of their giving should go to a need they can see—so that they understand the impact of their gift. One example would be buying food for a needy family they know.

Daryl and Kathy Heald have a passion for giving globally, and want to pass it on to their children. They had their children decorate a large "Missionary Jar" with pictures of people from around the world and place it in a prominent kitchen spot.

Every day the family puts their change in the jar. When they eat out, the children learn the concept of sacrificial giving by doing without a drink or dessert so that the money saved can be deposited in the jar. Then when missionaries visit their home, the children can choose to give them some or all of the money collected in the jar. They are learning that their giving helps people reach others for Christ throughout the world.

Taking your child on a mission trip to a developing country is a powerful experience. Exposure to desperate poverty can initiate a lifetime of giving to the poor. We also recommend a family time each week for dedicating that week's gifts to the Lord. The more involvement children have with their parents in giving, the more likely they are to develop into generous givers as adults.

LEARNING TO WORK

Parents also have responsibility to train children in the value and dignity of work. Consider these four areas in this training.

Learning routine responsibilities

The best way for a young child to become a faithful worker is to establish the habit of daily household chores. These are chores that each member of the family is expected to perform. For example, my daughter washed the dishes, and my son cleaned the kitchen.

Exposing your children to your work

Not too many years ago, most children were involved in earning the family's income. Today, however, that is seldom the case. Even so, exposing your children to what you do on your job is important in teaching them the value of work. If you own your own business, encourage your children to participate.

One word of advice: Because most children are no longer with their parents at work, parents' work habits *around the home* will be a major modeling influence. If a parent works hard at the office but complains about working at home, what is communicated to the children? Examine your work mindset and manner toward daily tasks at home to ensure that you are properly influencing your children. Earlier in this chapter I spoke of children soaking up parental attitudes like little sponges. Your facial expressions, eye-rolling, and under-the-breath groans will telegraph your real attitude more than all your well-chosen words. And so will a cheerful, optimistic frame of mind.

Earning extra money at home

Encourage your children to do extra work to earn money. A good rule of thumb is to pay them a fair wage for the work you would hire someone else to do. For example, if your car needs washing and your daughter needs some extra money, pay her to do it.

Working for others

A job gives a child an opportunity to enter into an employee-employer relationship. As children enter high school, discontinue allowances during the summer vacation to motivate them to earn money by holding a summer job.

It is wise for every child to experience a physically demanding job for at least one summer. Believe me, he or she will never forget it. I remember all too clearly the summer I worked at a lumber yard. Eight hours a day of lifting 40-pound bags of cement and loading trucks with lumber in the Florida heat and humidity was an unforgettable learning experience! Our daughter worked as a waitress, which was a priceless education in human nature.

"

The question to be asked at the end of an educational step is not 'What has the student learned?' but 'What has the student become?'" – President James Monroe

 PERSONAL REFLECTIONS

- Describe how you will train your children and/or help your grandchildren learn how to handle money God's way.

CHAPTER

OTHER FAMILY ISSUES

Experiencing other lifestyles

If children are constantly exposed to an affluent standard of living –
wealthy neighbors, private schools, and exclusive country clubs – they will
develop a distorted view of life. Parents must intentionally rupture this
insulated lifestyle by involving their children with people less fortunate.
Volunteering at a nursing home, participating with an inner-city ministry,
or delivering food to the homebound will give children an appreciation
for the financial realities of others and a more grateful heart for their own
abundance.

Ken and Meg Kendrick had a growing concern about the expectations
their children were developing because of their lifestyle. To help moderate
expectations, Ken and Meg made some changes: the family now does all
their own yard work, and they often fly coach and stay in economy motels
while traveling.

Overindulgence

When it comes to money, parents will frequently find themselves walking
a tightrope. Balance isn't easy! Yes, we can certainly tip toward being
miserly, but more often we are overindulgent. How many of us know

of a father who once sold newspapers to earn a bicycle and now has a 17-year-old son driving a sports car? Overindulgence saps the development of a child's character, essentially destroying the need for initiative. It creates in a child an expectation to be given things without giving anything in return.

Communicate that God has entrusted us with His money, that being good stewards includes guarding against waste. Teach them an *attitude of gratitude* by consistently expressing genuine thankfulness for all that the Lord has provided.

Teaching children the value of work builds their character. Not only do they gain more respect for the value of money and the effort required to earn it, a working child will be a more satisfied individual."

Selecting a spouse

One of the most crucial decisions children will ever make is the selection of a spouse. It is important to discuss this with them. Wealth makes a young adult an extremely attractive marital prospect.

Tim Case is the only child of a wealthy family. In college he fell in love with a classmate, Cindy, and they became engaged. It wasn't long, however, before a problem surfaced that ended the engagement. The next day Tim's roommate overhead Cindy saying to a friend, "The breakup with Tim is no big deal. There are lots of other rich guys to choose from."

Some girls attempt to trap wealthy young men in a sexual relationship; some men are single-minded in their search for an affluent young woman to marry. Advise your children not to discuss family finances with those they don't know well.

Here's an idea that may have fallen out of fashion: I believe *the family* should be involved in the courtship. One wise father invited his prospective son-in-law to join him on a variety of trips – business trips, mission trips, and vacations. The father wanted to spend one-on-one time with him to develop a close relationship, communicate his values, and assess the young man. After several months the father was satisfied that the young man would be a wonderful husband for his daughter and an asset to the family.

Become a coach.

As children leave home to marry, the role of the parents changes. No longer are their children subject to their authority. Genesis 2:24 says, *"A man will leave his father and mother and be united to his wife"* (NIV). During this season of life, parents should assume the role of coach, mentor, and encourager.

Bev and I have thoroughly enjoyed this relationship with our children and their spouses. I believe parents earn this role by expressing love and care to their children and their spouses in thoughtful and appropriate ways. Bev has been faithful to *"Train the younger women to love their husbands and children, to be self-controlled and pure, to be busy at home, to be kind, and to be subject to their husbands"* (Titus 2:4-5, NIV). In return, our daughter and daughter-in-law call Bev almost every day asking for advice – or just because they enjoy each other. I have focused on teaching our son-in-law and daughter-in-law how to handle money God's way.

Disclosure

Kevin and Jennifer questioned when they should disclose the extent of their assets to their children. Some trusts dictate when disclosure must occur. But when parents have flexibility, they can allow the maturity of the child to dictate the timing. Some can handle it well when they are 20; others need more time. This important issue requires parental discernment.

Grandparents

If you are a grandparent, you have a unique opportunity to influence your grandchildren. It is important for grandparents to play a complementary role in which they affirm the objectives of the parents. We recommend that the parents and grandparents schedule times together to discuss their training strategies – and how the grandparents can most effectively participate. This can greatly reduce the risk of bruised relationships and ineffective training.

Your story

My grandfather committed suicide when my father was only six years old. Until several years ago, I knew very little about his side of our family. I was thrilled to learn that my great grandfather was a pastor who served as a chaplain in the Civil War and later led a vibrant church.

In Deuteronomy 4:9, Moses wrote, *"Only give heed to yourself . . . so that you do not forget the things which your eyes have seen and they do not depart from your heart all the days of your life; but make them known to your sons and your grandsons."* Here's an idea you may not have considered: I strongly recommend that you write a letter or, better yet, produce a video in which you express to future generations your commitment to Christ, your life story, and the values that have shaped you. The Lord can use this in a very powerful way in the lives of those yet unborn. Encourage your children and their children – as we do ours – to continue this family tradition.

Your spouse

It can be challenging for the wealthy to enjoy a truly successful marriage. Wealth tends to breed an unhealthy sort of independence that can negatively affect the relationship. Many people believe that they *really can* buy happiness – a condominium here or a boat there. So when communication breaks down or a marital conflict surfaces, the husband can leave the country to hunt and the wife can go to a fitness camp.

Moreover, when one spouse brings a disproportionate amount of wealth into a marriage, it can present an unusual set of challenges. This is especially true when the wife is the recipient of great wealth and the husband is not a secure person. Because he may not be the provider for the family, he can feel that he receives less respect from his wife and children. In this circumstance, the wife needs to be particularly wise. When the husband makes a financial mistake, the wife must be careful not to say that he lost *her* money; it is *their* money.

Seeking counsel

One of the most simple and practical ways to nurture the marriage relationship is to consistently seek the advice of your spouse. Proverbs 19:20 reads, *"Listen to advice and accept instruction, and in the end you will be wise"* (NIV). And Proverbs 12:15 says, *"The way of a fool is right in his own eyes, but a wise man is he who listens to counsel."*

If the wife brings wealth into her marriage, she must be careful not to exclude her husband from financial meetings and decisions. Instead, she should consistently communicate that the money is *their* money, not just *hers*. In some situations, a wife may highly value her father's financial wisdom (if only she knew how many mistakes he made!). At the same time, however, she needs to seek her husband's counsel as a way of expressing admiration for him. Ephesians 5:33 reads, *"The wife must respect her husband"* (NIV). Few things undermine a husband more than the loss of his wife's admiration and respect.

On the other hand, if the husband brings the wealth to the marriage, the first person he needs to consult is his wife. Frankly, it has been a humbling experience for me to seek the counsel of my wife, Bev, in financial matters, because she has no formal financial training. But she has turned out to be my wisest counselor. Women tend to be gifted with a wonderfully sensitive and intuitive nature that is usually very accurate. Men tend to focus objectively on the facts. The husband and wife need each other to achieve the proper balance for optimal decisions. I also believe that the Lord honors the wife's "office" or "position" as helpmate to her husband. Many times the Lord communicates most clearly to the husband through his wife.

Husbands, let me be blunt. Regardless of her business background or her financial acumen or even her apparent disinterest, you must cultivate and seek your wife's counsel. The two of you should agree, because both of you will experience the consequences of any decision. Even if your choice proves to be disastrous, your relationship remains intact. There are no grounds for an "I told you so" response.

Prenuptial agreement

Generally, we do not recommend a prenuptial agreement. A husband and wife should be committed to one another for life, and such an agreement tends to undermine this trust relationship. Such an agreement, however, might be appropriate if a wealthy widow or widower with children remarries. The agreement can set forth how the estate will be distributed among the children. This can help the children relate to their new stepmother or stepfather in a healthier way because it eliminates questions of their new stepparent's motives – whether the stepparent is primarily interested in the children's surviving parent or in the family's money.

Parents and Siblings

Kevin's father was a poor Iowa farmer. Kevin was the third of five children in a very hard-working and close-knit family. From an early age, Kevin exhibited entrepreneurial drive. Later he worked his way through college, majoring in computer science. After graduation he founded a company that achieved enormous success within a few years. It was a truly remarkable achievement for the young man – but he was completely unprepared for the reaction of his family and friends

Some of his siblings became jealous and grew distant. They no longer felt comfortable socializing with him. Others communicated with him only when they wanted something. Kevin found himself increasingly isolated from his brothers and sisters.

Financial resources can be a wonderful blessing to a family. For example, money can buy excellent health care and a premium education. Even so, it would be shortsighted and foolish to ignore the challenges those resources present. Here are several of the more common ones.

Parents

Wealthy parents can not-so-subtly pressure their children to work for the family business – or involve themselves in pet projects or social organizations dear to the parents' heart.

Mike and Yolanda Brown believed their marriage of six years was successful except for one painful issue. Mike's domineering parents constantly interjected themselves and their strong opinions. Even though this was a major source of stress for Yolanda, Mike was reluctant to confront his parents for fear of losing their financial help. In fact, his wealthy parents were using money as a tool to control the young couple.

Mike was placing his parents above his wife, and from God's perspective this is a mistake. Jesus Christ said, *"A man shall **leave** his father and mother, and shall **cleave** to his wife"* (Matthew 19:5, emphasis added). When you marry, you are to leave your parents for your spouse in order to become financially, emotionally, and spiritually independent of them. Part of the reason God made it clear we should leave is because it forces us to mature and become more dependent on each other and our heavenly Father.

Bald eagles spend about two months building a nest for the mother to incubate her eggs. When a baby eagle is born, the parents feed and care for it until it reaches about twelve weeks of age – old enough to fly. Then the mother gently nudges the young eagle out of the nest, forcing it to use its little wings. Like eagles, parents should encourage their married children to transfer their dependence to the Lord and to each other.

This can be an emotional time for all concerned. Compare life to a book with a series of chapters that we open and close as we move from one phase to another. Closing some chapters takes courage and wisdom – and may even include some sorrow.

In this "Leaving" chapter, the parents' role changes to that of coaches or advisors. They should allow the young couple to make their own decisions – even if the choices aren't the ones the parents would make. (This doesn't preclude the parents from offering appropriate financial help.)

Children, on the other hand, should continue to honor their parents and seek their counsel without remaining emotionally or financially dependent on them. Husband and wife need to cleave to one another. In the original language the word for "cleave" literally means to "stick like glue." It's like two pieces of paper being glued together; you cannot separate them without tearing them both.[9]

Marriage experts Don and Sally Meredith emphasize the importance of this principle: "Just about every marriage problem stems from either a failure to *leave* or a failure to *cleave*." It can be helpful for couples to create lists describing the good and bad of parental involvement in their marriage. Try to identify everything that might have a bearing on how completely you have made the transition from "their home" to "your home."

Siblings

Sometimes tension between older siblings surfaces as one or more begin to patronize their affluent parents in order to receive a larger portion of the inheritance. Some may depend financially on their parents more than the others do. They may not have cut the cord emotionally, which can result in limiting their accomplishments.

In other families, one sibling may become wealthy while the rest do not. The affluent brother or sister may have a dramatically different lifestyle. This can create jealousy and even animosity. Expectations may be difficult to manage.

A sibling, for example, might ask you for a loan to purchase something you don't think would be good for them. Or they might approach you about investing in a business opportunity that doesn't appear wise.

Each case must be judged separately. The natural instinct is to help, but we should pray and attempt to discern the best way to help. Sometimes a gift of money is the right thing to do. At other times, this may not be the Lord's will. Instead of helping your brother or sister, you could find yourself getting in the way of what God wants to accomplish in their lives. At such times, your best gift to them might not be cash; you might benefit them more by helping them become better money managers or more faithful workers.

A successful restaurant chain owner has a sister who lives on welfare. Three times she has been on the verge of bankruptcy and three times he has rescued her. He paid off all her debt, purchased a debt-free home for her, and put adequate money in her saving account to provide for her needs. Less than five years after each bailout, she was back where she started. The fact is, her real need wasn't money at all, it was knowing how to control her spending.

In my experience, one of the major challenges with wealth in a family is unspoken expectations. Honest communication, difficult or awkward as that may be sometimes, is the only effective way to address expectations. I pray that the Lord will give you wisdom on the best way for your family members to meet and discuss openly the issues surrounding affluence.

✏ PERSONAL REFLECTIONS

- Describe some of the blessings your resources have allowed you to experience with family members.

- Describe some of the challenges your resources have caused with family members.

- What was the most helpful thing you learned from reading this chapter? How will you apply it?

16

WEALTH TRANSFER

Kevin and Jennifer Simmons had a will, and that was good. Their will, however, had become out of date, which wasn't good, and needed attention.

They realized they needed a new one and should discuss it with their children, but somehow, it never seemed like "the right time." The truth is, they were reluctant to think about details surrounding their deaths. They felt intimidated by the emotions this kind of family discussion might surface. So they procrastinated, and time slipped by.

But once Kevin and Jennifer came to grips with their need to be faithful stewards—in life *and* death – they were motivated to leave their resources in ways that would please the Lord.

Why do most affluent families struggle with matters concerning death and the transfer of wealth? Let's summarize some of the biggest challenges you will face:

- Providing for your spouse

- Helping your children and grandchildren financially without harming them

- Managing expectations of family members

- Dealing with sons-in-law, daughters-in-law, and step children

- Deciding what charities or ministries to support

- Avoiding family conflict and sibling jealousy

- Dealing with the reality of your death

- Understanding the complexities of wills, trusts, and estate taxes

Whew! Is it any wonder people put updating their wills at the bottom of their to-do lists?

Let's remind ourselves of these realities:

We all will die. As Isaiah told King Hezekiah, *"Thus says the Lord, 'Set your house in order, for you shall die'"* (2 Kings 20:1).

We will take nothing with us. *"And* [Job] *said, 'Naked I came from my mother's womb, and naked I will depart'"* (Job 1:21, NIV).

Someone else will get our stuff. *"I* [Solomon] *must leave it* [my possessions] *to the man who will come after me. And who knows whether he will be a wise man or a fool? Yet he will have control over all the fruit of my labor"* (Ecclesiastes 2:18-19).

Estate planning should be a spiritual exercise, not merely a financial or legal matter. We should work it out in the presence of God and to His glory. What a marvelous privilege God has granted us to select the next stewards. Looking at the big picture, you have only three choices for the next steward:

HEIRS — NONPROFIT ORGANIZATIONS — GOVERNMENT

- *Your heirs.* We will discuss leaving an inheritance to heirs in a moment.

- *Nonprofit organizations.* Although tax savings is not the primary goal, it is important to note that transferring wealth to a church or ministry is the most tax-efficient choice. Gifts to nonprofits currently are 100 percent deductible from your estate. Too many affluent people have not made provision in their will to fund the work of Christ.

- *Government.* Some people unintentionally make the government a large beneficiary by paying estate taxes they could have avoided or reduced through wise tax planning.

What the Bible says about leaving an inheritance

First, the Bible makes it clear that parents should leave an inheritance to their children and even their grandchildren. *"A good man leaves an inheritance to his children's children"* (Proverbs 13:22).

But God's Word also follows up on that statement with a powerful warning: *"An inheritance gained hurriedly at the beginning will not be blessed in the end"* (Proverbs 20:21). This represents one of the biggest challenges for the affluent. Henry Ford said, "Fortunes tend to self-destruction by destroying those who inherit them." Commodore Vanderbilt's grandson, heir to $60 million in 1885, observed, "Inherited wealth is as certain death to ambition as cocaine is to morality."

There is sobering evidence that inheritance often hurts the recipient. Studies show that the very *expectation* of an inheritance diminishes personal drive, saps motivation to work, and erodes life purpose. In addition, having a reason to look forward to the death of a loved one can have a devastating spiritual impact on one's soul.

How to make sure the inheritance will be a blessing.

Consider these suggestions to help ensure that the inheritance you leave for your children and grandchildren will be a blessing.

Train your heirs.

Remember that the younger generation must develop financial wisdom *before* they can manage wealth. Unfortunately, some parents purposely make money mysterious—or use it as a tool to control their children. You will actually have more influence over their behavior if you teach them how and why to handle money wisely. The worst thing you can do is to transfer wealth if you haven't first transferred wisdom.

Some parents have had the tendency to train their sons but not their daughters to handle money wisely. This is a tragic mistake. Parents must invest equal effort in training all their children.

Design wealth transfer to develop your heirs' character.

Some parents have designed incentives into their transfer of wealth to motivate their children to develop character, initiative, and work habits. Justin and Amy Connor crafted their will so each child could receive specified amounts for:

- the down payment on their first home,

- matching principal prepayments the children make toward their home mortgage,

- startup capital in their first two business ventures, and

- partially matching the annual salary they earn (including their spouse's if they are married).

The children will not inherit amounts other than the ones tied to these incentives.

Stan and Kay Watson decided to give each of their children their inheritance in the form of an investment in a startup business. They invested both finances and experienced counsel to assist their children. The businesses have done well, but most importantly, this has helped the children mature into remarkably responsible young people.

Evaluate the impact on your heirs.

Outstanding financial author Ron Blue recommends asking yourself three questions as you consider transferring wealth.

1. What is the worst thing that can happen if I transfer wealth to _____?

2. How serious is it?

3. How likely is it to occur?

Blue goes on to suggest repeating these questions from a positive perspective. "What is the best thing that can happen if I transfer wealth to _____?"

Ask the questions for each potential recipient, whether it involves a child, grandchild, or charity. If you want to distribute your assets responsibly, the answers to these questions are crucial.

A friend of mine, very concerned about being a good steward, questioned how much wealth to transfer to his grandchildren in comparison with what he might give to several ministries. His adult children really didn't need the money. His grandchildren, now young adults, had shown themselves to be very irresponsible with money.

When I asked him the question, "What is the worst thing that can happen if you transfer wealth to your grandchildren?" he looked up at me and replied, "God's resources would be wasted."

After reflecting for a minute, he answered the second question. "That's very serious." Then, without a moment's hesitation, he answered the third, "Knowing them, it's 100 percent likely to occur."

Answering these questions helped him to remove false guilt and feel confident about his plans to fund the work of Christ.

If we produce kids that are productive and content . . . it almost doesn't matter how much we leave them. If our children are consumptive and discontent, we won't be able to leave them enough." – Author Russ Crosson

Decide how much to give your heirs.

How much should you leave your children and grandchildren? This is a huge issue.

Assess how well the younger generation has been trained to handle money. Ask the three questions Ron Blue recommends. Then pray and seek counsel. If you are married, discuss this with your spouse. Take whatever time is necessary for the Lord to confirm His direction.

Affluent people have reached a wide variety of conclusions:

- Some have limited inheritance to college or vocational training, which is intended to equip their children to earn a living.

- Others have left sufficient resources to provide children with a start in life – but not so much that it will undermine hard work and character development.

- A minority believe that their children are wise and mature enough to trust them with large estates.

The amount may be different for each child.

Probably every parent of more than one child have asked themselves a question something like this: How can children coming from the same parents and living in the same environment be so *different?* Then, as children become adults, their values and lifestyles may diverge even more.

As you contemplate choosing the next stewards of your resources, you may realize that some of your children are much better equipped to handle wealth than are others. And at the same time, some have more genuine needs than others. For example, one daughter may have been divorced and left alone to raise four young children. Another daughter may own a very profitable business.

It is a righteous person who lives for the next generation." – Dietrich Bonhoeffer

We are to love our children equally, which often means helping them uniquely. They are unique in not only their character, values, commitment to Christ, and ability to deal with life but also in their vocation, health, and immediate family situation. These circumstances may influence how much you plan to leave each child and, as circumstances change, you may need to adjust your plan accordingly.

Leaving unequal amounts may be a difficult decision because it feels unfair. No one wants to be accused of playing favorites. Even so, we encourage you to ask for the Lord's guidance if you need to consider such action. Remember that the life situations that seem so hopelessly complicated to you and me, aren't difficult at all for the Lord of time and eternity. He knows every human heart, and He knows what lies in the future for each one of us.

Decide when to transfer.

The first two decisions of "to whom" and "how much" pave the way for the decision of "when."

Many people wait until after death to distribute their wealth. Others choose to distribute some while they live and the rest through a will. Consider these benefits for giving your heirs some of their inheritance while you are living.

An inheritance gained hurriedly in the beginning will not be blessed in the end" (Proverbs 20:21).

Giving now may be more timely for their needs.

Helping a young mother stay at home or enabling your children to send their kids to a Christian school may be much more beneficial than simply adding to their net worth when they are fifty or sixty.

One of the best things about giving money to your children (or grandchildren) is the opportunity to watch them use it to enrich their lives – an opportunity you would miss if you waited to distribute assets through your estate. Perhaps one of your children feels called to be a missionary. Would a financial gift from you help make this a reality? Your generosity toward your children, exercised with wisdom, can open doors and alleviate financial burdens when it comes to things like starting a business, buying a first home, or funding your grandchildren's college education.

Giving now will help train them.

If you want to include your children in your will but are unsure about their ability to handle money, consider giving them a "training" inheritance while you are alive.

When their four children reached their eighteenth birthdays, Brad and Ann gave them a small portion of their inheritance. Their goal was to find out how they would handle a small amount of money – and, consequently, how they would likely handle more.

The children, being young and inexperienced in financial management, wasted most of the money. But they learned valuable lessons from their mistakes. Today, Brad and Ann periodically give their children money, and the children do a masterful job of handling it wisely.

Brad and Ann are giving their children "hands on" experience. As we observed earlier, experience is a very good teacher, but coached experience is a *great* teacher. In other words, experience coupled with a mentor is of greater benefit. And you may be comforted to know that even though mistakes will be made with the money you provide now, those mistakes will help minimize larger ones with the amounts you leave at death.

Stay out of the way of God dealing with your children.

As beneficial as current giving to your children can be, it's not always God's will for you to solve their problems with money. God may have other lessons for them, including learning to trust Him for their provision. The more you have, the more difficult it is to allow your children to learn the fiscal discipline that comes from suffering the consequences of their mistakes. It is so much easier for you to "take away the pain"—just because you can. Knowing when to solve a problem with a check and when to allow God to deal with your children requires prayer and discernment.

Funding the work of God now

The same principles of deciding when to give apply to the work of Christ. Suppose your church or your favorite ministry has a current need to complete a God-directed mission. By waiting to give until after you die, you may have missed funding the most strategic opportunity for the ministry in your lifetime. As Ron Blue recommends, "Do your givin' while you're livin', so you're knowin' where it's goin'!"

The wealth-transfer family conference

If you are like most parents, you may very well feel uncomfortable discussing wealth-transfer plans with your children. Adult children are even less comfortable bringing up such issues. They may might have an honest desire to help, but how do you even start such a conversation without seeming nosy or greedy?

A family conference can provide tremendous benefits, including peace of mind. It gives your heirs the opportunity to hear from you – your heart, your wishes—in a comfortable setting free from outside distractions. It also gives family members permission to ask questions. Although parents still make the distribution decisions, such a conference promotes dialogue concerning these issues while all parties are present—rather than after a death, when most unplanned and emotionally stressful family conferences occur.

 Parents should wait until their children are old enough to understand the implications of such a conference. Some find it helpful to involve a facilitator, a trusted advisor to direct and mediate the discussion. Mom and Dad can explain their current estate plan. Together, the family can discuss amounts to be given to God's work and even help select the ministries. In such a setting, children have the opportunity to express honest feelings regarding the amounts their parents are leaving to them.

Most attorneys and financial professionals are trained to pass on as much money as possible to the next generation without considering the spiritual impact."

Avoiding these issues throughout life means more uncertainty, anxiety, and escalated conflict after the parents' death. The person who inherits may feel a sentimental obligation beyond anything the parents or grandparents intended. The inheritors may say irrational things like, "We can never sell that stock because Grandpa gave it to us and he never sold it."

John and Mary Rogers were in their seventies and were deeply committed to Christ. John's auto parts company had $300 million in annual sales. They had two married daughters.

The Rogerses asked their CPA to direct a family conference to discuss the transfer of the company to the girls. They spent hours talking about life goals and transfer plans. Mr. Rogers expressed his complete trust in the daughters' future stewardship of the company.

Suddenly the CPA asked the daughters a question. "Let's say your parents have been dead for five years. You have been running the company and it has done very well. A large publicly owned company approaches you with an offer of $500 million for the company. What are you going to do?"

Without a moment's hesitation, the younger daughter blurted, "Sell it!"

A brief, awkward silence followed. The CPA asked Mr. Rogers, "How do you feel about that?"

He repeated aloud, almost to himself, "Hmmm . . . I said I trusted them, didn't I?"

He thought a minute longer. "Then it must have been the right decision."

From that moment on, the daughters enjoyed the freedom to make any decisions in the best interest of the company – even a sale.

How often should I review my estate plan?

Experts recommend reviewing your plan every three years – perhaps sooner if you or your family have experienced significant changes. Keep in mind that wealth-transfer plans represent a process. As circumstances change, as ministry opportunities change, as tax laws change, and as you learn new information, you will want to review your plan.

First things first

First, decide *how you want to distribute* your assets and *how to prepare* your heirs for what they will receive. You should engage estate professionals to draw up documents only *after* you have made these basic decisions. Don't do it the other way around, because the professional may not clearly understand what you really want to accomplish. Most attorneys are trained to pass on as much money as possible to the next generation without considering the spiritual impact on the heirs.

Remember, it is an awesome privilege the Lord has given you to select the next stewards of the assets entrusted to you.

✏ PERSONAL REFLECTIONS

- Describe the process you have gone through (or will go through) to plan and document your estate.

- Describe your philosophy of leaving an inheritance to your children and grandchildren.

View the Chet and Diana Stewart – Trailers Behind the Hearse video (7:37) at ChartingYourLegacy.org, or by using this QR code.

- What was the most helpful portion of the video, and how will you apply it?

17

FINISHING WELL

The signature line would be waiting at the bottom of the contract. Scribbling the name his parents had given him fifty-two years earlier would give Rogers Kirven enough cash to have the freedom to do whatever he wanted. All he had to do the next day was sign. Then he could build the life of his dreams: more time with his wife and family, and daily options that didn't start with a trip to the office at the crack of dawn. All he had to do was sign.

"Tomorrow is the day," Rogers said to his two friends who had sold their companies a few years earlier. The trio met at a restaurant to celebrate the pending sale. It had been quite a while since they had seen each other, and Rogers walked in expecting a celebration and pats on the back.

But it didn't turn out that way.

"The first thing they told me," Rogers recalled, "was that they had new wives. I'd known one of them for fifteen years and another for seven. Both of them had cashed out to spend more time with the family." Over lunch, the conversation bounced around from their new homes to their skiing and golf, never once landing on anything meaningful.

Finally, Rogers asked his friend of fifteen years, also a follower of Christ, "Was this the best thing you ever did in your life?"

His friend shook his head in confusion and said, "I don't know. I don't think so."

Two hours later, Kirven Rogers walked out of the restaurant terrified.[10] But he had learned a powerful lesson.

These hard-working individuals had largely lost their zest for life. Their relationship with Christ had been too immature to tolerate this change and sudden wealth. In short, their character had not been sufficiently developed. Godly character is the key to finishing well.

Finishing well is rare.

In your journey with the Lord, it's not how you start that matters; it's how you finish. What are you doing to become the one in three who reaches the finish line still serving Christ? You will need spiritual discipline to have a strong finishing kick when you hit the tape at age 65, 75, 85, or whatever age God calls you home.

As author Steve Farrar said, "It's *endurance* that determines whether a person will finish strong. And endurance is the byproduct of godly character. The Christian life isn't a 100-yard dash; it's a marathon. Long races don't require speed; they require grit, determination, and finishing power."

As Scripture says, *"Therefore, since we have so great a cloud of witnesses surrounding us, let us also lay aside every encumbrance and the sin which so easily entangles us, and let us run with endurance the race that is set before us, fixing our eyes on Jesus"* (Hebrews 12:1-2).

Finish strong despite past mistakes.

Some football teams have a tradition of holding up four fingers at the beginning of the fourth quarter of each game, signifying their commitment to play hard to the end. The players may be fatigued, may have made earlier mistakes, may be bruised and battered, but they want to finish well.

On New Year's Day of 1929, Georgia Tech played the University of California in the Rose Bowl. A California player named Roy Riegels recovered a fumble. Somehow, he became disoriented and sprinted sixty-five yards – in the wrong direction! One of his teammates tackled him just before he crossed the wrong goal line. His mistake was made in the privacy of 80,000 screaming fans!

When the players filed off the field and went into their dressing rooms for half time, Roy Riegels put a towel over his head, sat in a corner, and wept uncontrollably.

When the timekeeper came in and announced that there were three minutes before the start of the second half, California coach Nibbs Price went over to Riegels and told him that he wanted him to start the second half. Riegels looked up with tear-filled eyes. "Coach," he said, "I can't do it. I've ruined you. I've ruined the University of California. I've ruined my teammates and myself."

Coach Price put his hand on Riegels' shoulder and said, "Roy, the game is only half over. Your team needs you now like it's never needed you before." Roy Riegels went back, and those Georgia Tech players will tell you that they had never seen a man play football as Roy Riegels played that second half. He was courageous, and he never gave up. He finished well.[11]

Finishing well does not mean finishing with a perfect record. But it does mean learning from our mistakes, getting back on course, and pursuing Christ with our whole heart. We are to work hard in building the kingdom of God as long as we are able, despite any previous mistakes we may have made.

As you read these words, you may think it's already too late for you to finish well. Perhaps you've made some big, bone-head mistakes, or squandered too many opportunities along the way. But here is the undeniable truth: Many of those who finished well in the Bible were guilty of terrible decisions. Abraham lied. Moses committed murder. David was an adulterer and a murderer. Peter denied Christ three times.

Paul, that former murderous persecutor of the early church said it this way: *"One thing I do: forgetting what lies behind and reaching forward to what lies ahead, I press on toward the goal for the prize of the upward call of God in Christ Jesus"* (Philippians 3:13-14).

Finish strong despite your age.

Aging is an inevitable part of life, and brings with it some unavoidable limitations. But we need to embrace God's perspective. As John Quincy Adams was nearing the end of his life, a friend asked how he was doing. "John Quincy Adams is well, quite well," replied the sixth President of the United States. "But the house in which he lives at present is becoming quite dilapidated. It's tottering upon its foundations. Time has nearly destroyed it. Its roof is pretty well worn out. It is becoming almost uninhabitable, and I think John Quincy Adams will have to move out of it soon. But he himself is quite well, quite well."

Old age is temporary – the decisive lap in the grand race of life. To finish well, we need to invest our life to its fullest in serving Christ during our time on earth." – Anonymous

The apostle Paul said it this way, *"For we know that if the earthly tent which is our house is torn down, we have a building from God, a house not made with hands, eternal in the heavens. For indeed in this house we groan, longing to be clothed with our dwelling from heaven"* (2 Corinthians 5:1-2).

As we age, we are encouraged to concentrate on developing a closer relationship with the Lord. *"Therefore we do not lose heart, but though our outer man is decaying, yet our inner man is being renewed day by day"* (2 Corinthians 4:16). George Fooshee has mentored me for more than three decades. George and his wife, Marjean, are in their late eighties. They are more in love with Christ and with each other than ever before. They continue to invest in the lives of others in their church, city, and around the world. The Psalmist wrote, *"The righteous will flourish like a palm tree . . . They will still bear fruit in old age, they will stay fresh and green"* (Psalm 92:12, 14, NIV).

Think of all those who have led enormously productive lives in old age. While in their eighties:

- Moses led the children of Israel out of captivity.

- Winston Churchill wrote his four-volume *A History of the English-Speaking Peoples*.

- "Colonel" Harland Sanders founded the Kentucky Fried Chicken (KFC) restaurant chain.

- Mother Teresa tirelessly served Calcutta's poor.

Not long ago, a small group of us met with an 85-year-old who has influenced scores of men and women in China for Christ. He told us of his sorrow, because his wife of more than sixty years had just died. For several years, he had been giving her around-the-clock care. Then he shared how the Lord recently had used him to lead a young girl to Christ. As he spoke, we were arrested by the love of Christ and the joy that radiated from his face.

When one of us asked, "What are your aspirations in this season of your life?" he answered without hesitation, "To take another mountain for God, just as Caleb did."

Old age is temporary – the decisive lap in the grand race of life. To finish well, we need to invest our life to its fullest in serving Christ during our time on earth.

CHALLENGES TO FINISHING WELL

To help us, in the following chapters we will address some of the most common reasons that wealthy followers of Christ do not finish well.

- A distorted view of retirement and leisure
- Not fulfilling God's calling
- Debt
- Dishonesty
- Marital dysfunction
- Not seeking counsel or having accountable relationships
- Not growing in their relationship with Christ

✏ PERSONAL REFLECTIONS

Read Revelation 3:21. *"To him who overcomes* [finishes well], *I* [Jesus] *will give him the right to sit with me on my throne, just as I overcame* [finished well] *and sat down with my Father on his throne."*

- What are some of the benefits you will experience in heaven if you finish well?

View the video – Schindler's List "Just One More" (2:56) at ChartingYourLegacy.org, or by using this QR code.

[Note: The main character in this film is Oskar Schindler, a compassionate German businessman who ransoms 1,100 Jews from the death camps during World War II. In this scene the war has just been declared over, and he is surrounded by those he saved.]

• What did you learn from this video? How will you apply it?

18

CHALLENGE OF RETIREMENT AND LEISURE

Before we address retirement, it will be helpful to understand God's perspective on work. It was initiated for our benefit in the sinless environment of the garden of Eden. *"The LORD God took the man and put him into the garden of Eden to cultivate it and keep it"* (Genesis 2:15).

Think about it. The very first thing the Lord did with Adam was to hand him a shovel. He put him to work!

After the Fall when sin entered the earth, however, work became exponentially more difficult. *". . . Cursed is the ground because of you; in toil you will eat of it all the days of your life. Both thorns and thistles it shall grow for you; and you will eat the plants of the field; by the sweat of your face you will eat bread"* (Genesis 3:17-19).

Work is so important that in Exodus 34:21 God gives this command: *"You shall work six days."* The apostle Paul is just as direct: *"If anyone is not willing to work, then he is not to eat"* (2 Thessalonians 3:10). Examine this verse. It does not apply to those who are physically or mentally unable to work; it is for those who are able but choose not to work.

One of the primary purposes of work is to develop character. While the carpenter is building a house, the house is also building the carpenter. The carpenter's skill, diligence, manual dexterity, and judgment are refined. A job isn't just a task designed to earn money; it's also intended to produce godly character in the life of the worker.

Retirement! Years of leisure – resting, playing, and traveling. The mindset of our peers is that we must reward ourselves now in this life for our years of labor. But what a strange reward for a Christian to set his sights on while living in the midst of millions of people faced with an eternity separated from Christ. What a tragic way to finish our last mile before entering the presence of the King who finished his last mile so differently!"
– Author John Piper

We work for . . . .

Did you know that in our work we actually serve the Lord rather than people? Paul writes: *"Whatever you do, do your work heartily, as for the Lord rather than for men . . . It is the Lord Christ whom you serve"* (Colossians 3:23-24, emphasis added). The most important question we need to answer every day as we begin our work—whatever the task might be—is this: "For whom do I work?" The Bible makes it clear: No matter where you are or what you do, no matter who signs your paycheck, you ultimately work for Christ Himself. Recognizing that we work for the Lord enables us to grow closer to Him.

We are to work hard and get adequate rest.

"Whatever your hand finds to do, do it with all your might" (Ecclesiastes 9:10, NIV). *". . . The precious possession of a man is diligence"* (Proverbs 12:27).

Scripture encourages hard work and diligence, while laziness is strongly condemned: *"He who is slack in his work is brother to him who destroys"* (Proverbs 18:9). Hard work, however, must be balanced by the other priorities of life, including adequate rest and recreation. The Lord memorialized resting one day out of seven in the Ten Commandments.

> *"Remember the Sabbath day, to keep it holy. Six days you shall labor and do all your work, but the seventh day is a sabbath of the Lord your God; in it you shall not do any work, you or your son or your daughter, your male or your female servant or your cattle or your sojourner who stays with you. For in six days the Lord made the heavens and the earth, the sea and all that is in them, and rested on the seventh day"* (Exodus 20:8-11).

Consider this commandment more closely: It is the longest of the Ten Commandments; it calls the Sabbath holy; and it's the only one that God applies to Himself. Many followers of Christ believe the other nine commands apply to them, but somehow feel that a day of rest was only applicable in the Old Testament.

When you think about it, rest can easily become an issue of faith. Is the Lord able to make our six days of work more productive than seven? Of course He is! For example, Hobby Lobby and Chick-fil-A are two large businesses founded by followers of Christ that have never been open on Sunday. Yet they have prospered.

Exodus 34:21 reads, *"You shall work six days, but on the seventh day you shall rest; even during plowing time and harvest you shall rest."* Our Creator instituted weekly rest for our physical, mental, and spiritual health.

Retirement

Our culture promotes the goal of retirement to pursue a life filled with leisure. Is this a biblical goal? In the parable of the rich fool, Jesus strongly rebukes the notion of a life of leisure and ease: *"I [the rich fool] will say to my soul, 'Soul, you have many goods laid up for many years to come; take your ease, eat, drink and be merry.' But God said to him, 'You fool!'"* (Luke 12:19-20). A proper amount of time spent on leisure is important and pleases God, but it's unhealthy if it becomes the focus of our life.

Numbers 8:24-26 is the only reference to retirement in the Bible, and it applied specifically to the Levites working in the tabernacle. I don't want to jump to conclusions here, but I'm guessing not too many of us are Levities serving in the tabernacle these days!

While people are physically and mentally capable, there is no scriptural basis for retiring and becoming unproductive – the concept of putting an older, able person "out to pasture." Don't let age stop you from finishing the work God has called you to accomplish. He will provide you with the necessary strength and mental acuity.

The Bible does imply, however, that the type or intensity of labor may change as we grow older, shifting gears to a less demanding pace to become more like the "elder seated at the gate" or the *"older women . . . [who] can urge the younger women to love their husbands and children, to be self-controlled and pure . . ."* (Titus 2:3-5). During this season of life, we can use the experience and wisdom gained over a lifetime. If we have sufficient income to meet our needs apart from our business and jobs, we may choose to transition from our career early to invest more time in serving others.

Carefully read what Peter said toward the end of his life.

> *"I consider it right, as long as I am in this earthly dwelling, to stir you up by way of reminder, knowing that the laying aside of my earthly dwelling is imminent, as also our Lord Jesus Christ has made clear to me. And I will also be diligent that at any time after my departure you may be able to call these things to mind"* (2 Peter 1:13-15).

Do the words *"stir you up"* and *"diligent"* give even the slightest hint of retirement? On the contrary, they communicate an active life.

Greg dropped out of college after his freshman year and soon started a business selling pizza out of the trunk of his car. When he was in his mid-forties he enrolled in what became the Compass *Charting Your Legacy* small group study while in the midst of selling his business to a Fortune 500 company for $100 million. For twenty-five years, he had shouldered the responsibility and stress of building his company without really having sufficient capital. His objective was to sell out and enjoy a relaxed life with plenty of time for golf.

During the study, however, Greg found himself challenged to rethink those plans. He discovered that the Lord discouraged retirement, so he began praying for the Lord to show him what he should do. I'll never forget his excitement when he came to class and announced what he sensed God wanted him to do: Build businesses so that by the time he died, the enterprises would be giving $1 million each *day* to the work of Christ!

I don't know if Greg will achieve this God-sized dream. But I do know that he is engaged like never before in an exciting walk of faith with Christ. He is having a massive influence on his 700 employees and funding ministries around the world that serve needy women and children.

Toward the end of his life, the apostle Paul had to make a similar decision. *"Now, compelled by the Spirit, I am going to Jerusalem, not knowing what will happen to me there. I only know that in every city the Holy Spirit warns me that prison and hardships are facing me. However, **I consider my life worth nothing to me, if only I may finish the race and complete the task the Lord Jesus has given me**"* (Acts 20:22-24, NIV, emphasis added).

Paul could have disobeyed the Lord to pursue a safer, more comfortable life. After all he had suffered as an apostle, he might have put his feet up in some Mediterranean villa, sipping on a cool drink and watching the clouds float by. But he had seen the risen Christ face-to-face, and that experience had changed him forever. It was infinitely more important to him to faithfully complete his God-given task – even if that meant the certainty of prison and the risk of death.

✏ PERSONAL REFLECTIONS

View the John Piper video – *You Have One Life, Don't Waste it* (7:29), by visiting ChartingYourLegacy.org or by using this QR code:

- What was the most motivating part of the video?

- How did it influence your perspective of retirement?

CHAPTER

19

CHALLENGES TO FINISHING WELL – FULFILLING YOUR CALLING

Through the years, we have encountered questions like these again and again: What should I do for the rest of my life? Should I sell my business and become a full-time volunteer at my church or in a ministry? Should I focus on my business to produce even more funds for the work of Christ? I've invested much of my time in raising our children and soon we'll be empty nesters. What should I do now?

One of the purposes of this chapter is to provide you a framework to help you identify your calling. *A "calling" is the primary task or vocation God intends for you. It is the overarching purpose for you as an individual.*

You have a calling.

Never doubt it: The Lord intends for us to fulfill a specific calling or purpose. Ephesians 2:10 reads, *"For we are His workmanship, created in Christ Jesus for good works, which God prepared beforehand, that we should walk in them."*

Just as God gave you unique fingerprints, you have been created like no one else in human history. At your conception, God created a new DNA that has never been before and will never be again."

Study this passage carefully. *"We are His workmanship."* Another translation says, *"We are His handiwork"* (AMP). Each of us has been uniquely created and given special physical, emotional, and mental characteristics and abilities. Just as God gave you unique fingerprints, you have been created like no one else in human history. At your conception, God created a new DNA that has never been before and will never be again.

The passage continues, *"created in Christ Jesus for good works, which God prepared beforehand, that we should walk in them"* (Ephesians 2:10). The Lord created each of us for a particular task, and He endowed us with the skills, aptitudes, and desires to accomplish this work.

Most of us struggle with too many things to do and too little time in which to do them. The good can become the enemy of the best. Once we have a clear understanding of God's call on our life, it becomes much easier to evaluate opportunities and say "No" to those that would distract us from what the Lord wants us to accomplish.

I have two close friends. One has only average ability, but because he has been single minded in his focus, he has had an enormous impact. The other is much more gifted, but has scattered his energies by pursuing too many projects with limited success. Knowing your calling helps you focus and become more productive.

Fulltime Christian work or a secular job

Your calling may be to a fulltime Christian vocation or to a secular workplace. Many feel they aren't serving Christ in a significant way if they remain in business – that only the missionary or pastor is truly "spiritual." Nothing could be further from the truth.

In his book, *God Owns My Business*, Stanley Tam writes, "Although I believe in the application of good principles in business, I place far more confidence in the conviction that I have a call from God. I am convinced that His purpose for me is in the business world. My business is my pulpit."

To those who earn their living through secular pursuits, it is a great comfort to know that the "call" of holy vocation carries over to all walks of life. First Corinthians 10:31 says it this way, "*. . . whatever you do, do it all to the glory of God*" (NIV). God strategically places His children everywhere, and we're to glorify Him wherever He chooses for us to work.

I know.

I'm a product of the marketplace.

As I mentioned in an earlier chapter, I began my career in Orlando and started meeting with a group of businessmen to learn how to be more effective in business. They were vibrant followers of Christ who used the platform of their companies to influence people like me. Though I had no interest in attending a church, their lives impressed me deeply. Within six months of regularly meeting with these men, I was introduced to Jesus Christ as my savior.

Men and women in the marketplace have the priceless opportunity to impact their customers, vendors, fellow workers, and even competitors for the Lord. And they also perform the vital function of providing financial and prayer support to the church and ministries.

Identifying Your Calling

Our primary calling at some stages of life may be obvious. For example, raising children for a young homemaker is a calling. But it's important for you to understand that God is at work around you as you seek to identify your calling. Consider this:

God prepares us.

God providentially allows us to experience circumstances to prepare us for our calling. God has been grooming you your entire life through your family, education, work, and your relationships. You may find this hard to believe, especially if these weren't godly influences. Some of these experiences were positive and others were difficult. For example, the Lord might use a painful divorce to give someone the empathy and passion to serve others in similar situations.

God calls us.

God communicates to each of us in a personal, unique way. Why? Because He wants us to experience Him as the living Lord, rather than following some technique or set of rules. He spoke to Moses through a burning bush, but as far as we know, He never spoke to anyone that way again. He appeared to the apostle Paul as a blinding light from heaven—a radiance so intense it slammed him to the ground. But that experience was never repeated in the New Testament, with Paul or anyone else.

It is unusual for the Lord to speak to us as He did to Moses from something as spectacular as a burning bush. He will, however, usually give us a passion for our calling and confirm our direction through circumstances and the Scriptures.

For six months I prayed, asking the Lord whether He wanted me to start a financial ministry, or to continue in the real estate development business. Then, someone I deeply admired urged me to begin what has become Compass.

The reason the Lord does not reveal many details about our calling is because He wants us to enter into an intimate walk of faith with Him."

The next morning, I asked the Lord if this person's counsel was from Him. Immediately the Holy Spirit unmistakably impressed on my mind Esther 4:14, *"And who knows whether you have not* [been called] *for such a time as this?"* This was the same passage He had originally given me when I was in the early stages of studying the biblical principles of finance. I knew with certainty that Christ was calling me to start a financial ministry.

God provides what is necessary.

God will provide what you need and when you need it to accomplish your calling.

An example of this provision is when the Lord sent Nathan the prophet to confront King David for his adultery with Bathsheba and the murder of her husband: *"... This is what the LORD, the God of Israel, says: 'I anointed you king over Israel, and I delivered you from the hand of Saul. I gave your master's house to you ... I gave you all Israel and Judah. And **if all this had been too little, I would have given you even more**'"* (2 Samuel 12:7-8, NIV, emphasis added).

God often provides few details.

Examine what Jesus said to the disciples when He called them, *"As Jesus was walking by the sea of Galilee, He saw two brothers, Simon, who was called Peter, and Andrew his brother, casting a net into the sea; for they were fishermen. And He said to them, 'Follow Me, and I will make you fishers of men'"* (Matthew 4:18,19).

Think of those the Lord called: Abraham, David, Jeremiah, Paul, and others. How many details were they initially given? Not many!

Though in some cases God gives more details than in others, in every case the individual must stay close to God for daily guidance. Usually, the Lord has a simple reason for not revealing too many details to us about our calling: He wants us to enter into an intimate, step-by-step walk of faith with Him. Without a close relationship with Christ, you will miss what He wants to do in and through you. He is more likely to ask you to follow Him one day at a time than He is to spell out all the details before you begin to obey Him.

Don't be surprised if it's out of your comfort zone! Consider the people God used in the Bible. God called almost all of them to step outside their comfort zone. Way outside!

For example, the Lord asked Abraham to leave his home for an unknown location; Moses to lead two million people through the Red Sea; Gideon to lead a band of 300 against a vast army; David to fight the nine-foot-tall giant Goliath; Daniel to spent a night in the lion's den; the engaged virgin Mary to give birth to the Savior.

I believe that the Lord delights in doing things through us that totally surprise us. There is no explanation for what is happening – except for God alone. This is true in my experience. When I started Crown in 1985 and then Compass in 2009, I never could have imagined that we would be teaching millions of people around the world each year.

Your calling requires obedience.

In Henry Blackaby's outstanding *Experiencing God* small group study, he points out, "Through your relationship with Jesus Christ, God reveals His will and invites you to join Him where He is already at work. When you obey, God accomplishes through you something that only He can do."

Psalm 127:1 says it this way, *"Unless the Lord builds the house, they labor in vain who build it."* If we want our lives to count for eternity, we must be rooted in willingness to follow and obey Christ wherever He chooses to lead us.

In fact, Jesus tells us that our obedience is evidence that we love Him. *"If you love me, you will obey what I command"* (John 14:15, NIV). *"Whoever has my commands and obeys them, he is the one who loves me. He who loves me will be loved by my Father, and I too will love him and show myself to him"* (John 14:21, NIV).

In the book of John, the inner life and motivations of Christ are revealed. His complete obedience and submission to the Father are made clear.

- *"I can do nothing on My own initiative. As I hear, I judge; and My judgment is just, because I do not seek My own will, but the will of Him who sent me"* (John 5:30).

- *"For I have come down from heaven, not to do My own will, but the will of Him who sent Me"* (John 6:38).

Jesus modeled obedience, and His supreme example is found in Philippians 2:8: *"And being found in appearance as a man, he humbled himself and became obedient to death – even death on a cross!"* (NIV)

At the end of his earthly ministry, Jesus measured success by the disciples who obeyed God's Word: *"I have revealed you to those whom you gave me out of the world. They were yours; you gave them to me and they have obeyed your word"* (John 17:6, NIV). He knew that making obedient disciples was critical if there were to be generations of vibrant followers impacting the world. Exponential growth of the kingdom was dependent upon it.

Take a moment and think about the importance of being obedient to the Lord and the willingness to follow Him. If you have any reservation, ask Him to work in your heart and give you the desire to be willing. He will hear you. It is a prayer He delights to answer.

Challenges

Everyone who responds to God's calling experiences challenges. These are intended to strengthen our faith in Christ, test our obedience, and develop godly character. There are a wide variety of challenges: financial, health, unfair treatment, and strained relationships with others.

David's initial challenge came in facing the giant Goliath. David responded courageously, recognizing that it was the Lord who was fighting for him: *"You come to me with a sword, a spear, and a javelin, but I come to you in the name of the LORD of hosts, the God of the armies of Israel, whom you have taunted. This day the LORD will deliver you up into my hands"* (1 Samuel 17:45-46).

✏ PERSONAL REFLECTIONS

- Do you know God's calling on your life? If so, how would you describe it? If you don't know your calling, what are you most passionate about in this season of your life?

- Describe your dominant abilities.

- Who could serve you as a trusted counselor to help you identify your calling?

CHALLENGES OF DEBT & DISHONESTY

Russell Ball and James Diaz are real estate developers who made a fortune during the real estate bubble of 2003-2006. Lenders were begging both of them to borrow money. But when the Great Recession slammed real estate, that's when their similarities ended.

Russell had borrowed millions to renovate his residence, buy a pricey vacation home, and launch more heavily leveraged real estate projects. James learned what the Bible said about debt, and paid off his home and business.

For the next five years, Russell spent most of his time squabbling with the formerly friendly lenders trying to avoid bankruptcy. James focused on buying real estate projects for pennies on the dollar. One of these men scrambled for financial survival; the other prospered.

Debt is discouraged throughout the Bible. Read the first portion of Romans 13:8 from several Bible translations: *"Owe no man anything"* (KJV). *"Let no debt remain outstanding"* (NIV). *"Pay all your debts"* (TLB). *"Owe nothing to anyone"* (NASB). *"Keep out of debt and owe no man anything"* (AMP).

In Proverbs 22:7, we learn why the Lord discourages debt: *". . . the borrower is slave to the lender"* (NIV). When we are in debt, we are slaves – to our lenders. The more debt we have, the heavier our chain of financial slavery becomes.

Debt considered a curse

In the Old Testament, being out of debt was one of the promised rewards for obedience. *"If you diligently obey the* LORD *your God, being careful to do all His commandments which I command you today, the* LORD *your God will set you high above all the nations of the earth. All these blessings shall come upon you and overtake you if you obey the* LORD *your God . . . you shall lend to many nations, but you **shall not borrow**"* (Deuteronomy 28:1-2, 12, emphasis added).

On the other hand, debt was one of the curses inflicted for disobedience. *"But it shall come about, if you do not obey the* LORD *your God, to observe to do all His commandments and His statutes with which I charge you today, that all these curses will come upon you . . . The alien who is among you shall rise above you higher and higher, but you will go down lower and lower. **He shall lend to you**, but you shall not lend to him"* (Deuteronomy 28:15,43-44, emphasis added).

Many people think borrowing is inevitable and don't bother developing strategies for themselves, their businesses, or investments to become debt free. And as we all have seen, the more debt we have, the more vulnerable we become to an unexpected economic downturn.

The decision to borrow is often based on the presumption that our investments or business will be profitable--or that our job will continue in the future.

The operative word there is *presumption.*

As we learned in an earlier chapter, James 4:13-14 cautions us against a presumptive attitude: *"Come now, you who say, 'Today or tomorrow we will go to such and such a city, and spend a year there and engage in business and make a profit.' **Yet you do not know what your life will be like tomorrow**"* (emphasis added). Proverbs 27:1 echoes this truth, *"Do not boast about tomorrow, for you do not know what a day may bring forth."*

While the Bible itself is silent about when we can borrow money, I recommend this rule of thumb:

Borrow as little as possible and pay it off as quickly as possible!

David Price is an extraordinary entrepreneur. He started two businesses from scratch and built them into enterprises, each worth $200 million. Sadly, he lost both businesses by encumbering them with too much debt.

When mountain climbers scale a steep face of rock, they often use a technique called "tying the knots." They will climb about ten feet, hammer a spike securely in the rock, and tie their supporting rope to the spike. They do this as a safety precaution. If they slip and fall, they will fall no farther than ten feet and are usually unharmed. If, however, climbers neglect to tie the knots, a single slip can drop them a long, long way down the cliff, resulting in serious injury or even death.

The concept of tying the knots is applicable to business and personal debt. When you pay off the debt on an asset, tie the knot! Avoid encumbering the free and clear asset in case a financial slip occurs.

Generally, there are two stages of borrowing.

Stage 1. You personally guarantee the debt.

When you are launching a business or it's not financially strong or you are making a high loan-to-value investment, lenders generally require you to personally guarantee the debt. When you personally endorse a debt, you pledge all your assets as collateral. Many people personally guarantee these debts and don't realize that as long as the debt exists, everything they own is at risk. Proverbs 22:26-27 paints this word picture: *"Do not be among those who give pledges, among those who become guarantors for debts. If you have nothing with which to pay, why should he take your bed from under you?"* Look at this passage. "DO NOT. . .." The Bible isn't make a suggestion here. This is a command!

We recommend establishing a goal that many would consider radical – that your cash rather than your ability to borrow be a governor on your lifestyle, investments, and business deals. One of your "boundaries in an ocean of choices" should be what you can afford without using debt."

Stage 2. The collateral is sufficient to borrow without a personal guarantee.

Work toward eliminating the need to personally guarantee debts. The lender should understand that the only security for the debt is the business or investments and anything else you are pledging as collateral. You have the option of paying the debt either with cash or with the assets pledged as collateral. The lender, then, has a decision to make: Do I feel good enough about the collateral to loan the money? This eliminates risking all your other assets.

Cosigning

Anytime you cosign, you become legally responsible for the debt of another. It's just as if you borrowed the money and gave it to your friend or relative who is asking you to cosign. In effect, *you* promise to pay back the entire amount if the borrower does not.

A Federal Trade Commission study found that 50 percent of those who cosigned for bank loans ended up making the payments. Those are pretty good odds that if you cosign, you'll pay.

Fortunately, the Bible gives us clear direction about cosigning. Proverbs 17:18 says, *"It is poor judgment to countersign another's note, to become responsible for his debts"* (NLT). The words "poor judgment" are literally translated "destitute of mind"!

Parents often cosign for their child's first automobile. We decided not to do this. We wanted to model for our children the importance of not cosigning and to discourage them from using debt. Instead, we encouraged them to think ahead and save for the purchase of their first cars.

Anytime you cosign, you become legally responsible for the debt of another."

Challenges to Finishing Well – Dishonesty

James Arnett's company invested hundreds of thousands of dollars in a proposal to develop a large government-owned parcel of land. His staff discovered that the other companies competing for the project had been holding private, illegal discussions with the city commissioners who were going to award the project.

James's staff asked his permission to initiate discussions with the commissioners. Without hesitation, James responded, "I'd rather lose ten times the money we've invested in the proposal than do anything that would compromise our integrity!" James's company lost the competition, but his honesty gained the respect of his employees and influenced some of them to consider Christ as their Savior.

There are hundreds of verses in the Bible that communicate the Lord's desire for us to be completely honest. This is a small sample:

- *"For the Lord your God detests anyone . . . who deals dishonestly"* (Deuteronomy 25:16, NIV).

- *"You shall not steal, nor deal falsely, nor lie to one another"* (Leviticus 19:11).

- *"The Lord loathes all cheating and dishonesty"* (Proverbs 20:23, TLB).

- *"Lying lips are an abomination to the Lord"* (Proverbs 12:22).

- *"The Lord hates . . . a lying tongue"* (Proverbs 6:16-17).

Look at the following comparison between what the Scriptures teach and what our society practices concerning honesty.

ISSUE	SCRIPTURE	SOCIETY
Standard of honesty:	Complete honesty	Changes with circumstances
God's concern about honesty:	He requires it	There is no god or he looks the other way
The decision to be honest or dishonest is based upon:	Faith in the invisible, living God	Only facts can be seen
Question usually asked when deciding whether or not to be honest:	Will it please God?	Will I get away with it?

Truthfulness is one of God's attributes. *"I am . . . the truth"* (John 14:6). He commands us to reflect His honest and holy character: *"Be holy yourselves also in all your behavior; because it is written, 'You shall be holy, for I am holy'"* (1 Peter 1:15-16).

In contrast to God's nature, John 8:44 describes the devil's character: *"He [the devil] was a murderer from the beginning, and does not stand in the truth because there is no truth in him. Whenever he speaks a lie, he speaks from his own nature, for he is a liar and the father of lies."* The Lord wants us to conform to His honest character rather than to the dishonest nature of the devil.

Have you ever thought about this? When we are dishonest, we are acting as if the living God doesn't even exist! By our actions, we are declaring that God isn't able to provide exactly *what* we need *when* we need it, even though He has promised to do so. *"But seek first his kingdom and his righteousness, and all these things* [food and clothing] *will be given to you as well"* (Matthew 6:33, NIV). When we decide to take things into our own hands and do them in our own dishonest way, we act as if God is incapable of discovering our dishonesty and that He is powerless to discipline us. If we really believe God will discipline us, then we won't consider acting dishonestly.

Honest behavior is often an issue of faith. An honest decision may look foolish in light of what we can see, but the godly person knows that Jesus Christ is alive even though He is invisible to us. Every honest decision strengthens our faith in the living God and helps us grow into a closer relationship with Christ. However, if we choose to be dishonest, we essentially deny our Lord and violate the greatest commandment. *"You shall love the Lord your God with all your heart, and with all your soul, and will all your mind"* (Matthew 22:37). It is impossible to love God like this if, at the same time, we are dishonest and act as if He doesn't exist.

Consider this: Jesus is the truth. He is holy, and no lie is found in Him. And He lives in you. When we submit to Christ, allowing Him to live His life through us, we are going to be absolutely honest.

✏ PERSONAL REFLECTIONS

- Describe the most difficult time you have had personally or in business because of debt.

- If you are in debt right now, do you have a strategy to get out of it? If you have a plan, describe it.

- Are you consistently honest in even small details? If not, what will you do to change?

RECOMMENDED RESOURCES

The book "HONESTY - A missing key to unlocking intimacy with God" by Howard Dayton. Order at compass1.org.

CHALLENGES TO FINISHING WELL – MARITAL DYSFUNCTION

Ron Phillips flew into a rage . . . again. "Don't you read your Bible?" he yelled at his wife, Jodi, pounding the dining room table. "God put the husband – not the wife – in charge. I'm the boss. You're supposed to submit to me and do whatever I tell you! I earn the money around here, and if I want to buy a new plane, God says I can do it. So, keep your nose out of our finances."

Jodi responded angrily, "Go ahead and get your plane! I'm sure it will impress your buddies next time you go hunting together. I'm out of here! My friends and I will be hanging out at the resort and spa for a couple of weeks. See ya!"

Here is the biggest lesson I've learned after counseling hundreds of couples: arguments over money usually aren't arguments over money. Something else in the marriage relationship is fractured, and financial issues are symptoms of the deeper problems. Most often the solution is simply for the husband and wife to fulfill their biblical roles in marriage.

The most important role for the husband is found in Ephesians 5:25.

"Husbands, love your wives, just as Christ loved the church and gave himself up for her" (NIV).

Don't skim over this verse. Examine it carefully.

Husbands are to love and sacrificially serve their wives the same way that Jesus loved and sacrificed Himself for the church. I first recognized this responsibility when writing the book *Money and Marriage God's Way,* and it revolutionized our marriage.

At about the same time, I met with a godly friend. He hadn't gotten much sleep the night before, and when I asked why, he chuckled. "Well, about two a.m. my wife woke me because she wasn't feeling well and wanted something from the all-night pharmacy. I never did get back to sleep."

"Bummer," I said.

"No," he smiled, "I never think of occasions like that as a nuisance. To me, they're opportunities to serve. If you don't remember anything else I ever tell you, remember to view every request by your wife as an opportunity to serve her."

For the past ten years, I've applied those words. *View every request by your wife as an opportunity to serve her!*

At first, it was difficult for me. I would smile and say "yes" to her request, but I was grumbling on the inside. However, after just a few months, I was surprised to experience joy when serving her. Now, I love serving her!

I am convinced that the Lord hardwired husbands to sacrificially serve their wives. When we do, the Holy Spirit – who lives in us – will allow us to experience His pleasure.

When Bev asked me to do something for her, if possible, I would stop what I was doing and immediately do it. And I discovered that this communicated to her that she was my priority. She was more important than my work, friends, or recreation.

All this was in preparation for a five-year journey as her care giver that started with a double mastectomy. The cancer then spread to her bones and finally her liver. Not once did I feel badly when she asked me to do something. It was the hardest time in our marriage, and it was the sweetest time in our marriage.

Then, a few weeks before she went Home to be with the Lord, a friend gave me priceless advice. He told me that when I went into her room, it was a sacred event. I was on holy ground. And that I should invite the Holy Spirit to love her through me.

And then, after only a few days, something happened. Our love became so much deeper, so much sweeter. I concluded that the Holy Spirit can love our spouse in ways that we cannot.

Let's shift gears and examine one of the key roles for wives as revealed in Ephesians 5:33, "*. . . the wife must respect her husband*" (NIV).

God designed wives to need love, and husbands to need respect. *Each one of you* [husbands] *also must love his wife as he loves himself, and the wife must respect her husband*" (Ephesians 5:33, NIV). He commanded husbands to love their wives unconditionally – no matter what – even when their wives do not obey the command to respect them. And wives must respect their husbands without condition – no matter what – even when their husbands fail to love them. There is no justification for a husband to say, "I will love my wife *after* she respects me," or for the wife to say, "I will respect my husband *after* he loves me."

Author Emerson Eggerich observes, "When a husband feels disrespected, he has a natural tendency to react in ways that feel unloving to his wife. When a wife feels unloved, she has a natural tendency to react in ways that feel disrespectful to the husband. Without love, she reacts without respect. Without respect, he reacts without love."

"Now here is the good news: When a wife respects her husband in ways that are meaningful to him, it ignites in him the feeling of love for his wife. Her deepest need – to feel loved – is satisfied. And when the husband loves his wife in ways that are meaningful to her, she responds with respect – meeting his greatest need."

Only in the Scriptures do we find out how to live in a way that pleases God and is, as a by-product, the most fulfilling for us."

Marital Infidelity

A well-known entrepreneur from the Midwest started with an initial investment of a few hundred dollars and built a company worth more than $100 million. He was generous and an outspoken follower of Christ. His wife and children also were committed to the Lord.

Then, the unthinkable happened. He became sexually involved with a younger woman at work, and the repercussions were horrendous. An emotional and highly contested divorce ensued after thirty-five years of marriage. The children chose sides and now refuse to communicate with one another. The business suffered because the husband and wife each owned 50 percent of the stock. His Christian testimony in the community was decimated.

One of his business associates observed, "Some of the most potent and dangerous aphrodisiacs are wealth, position, and fame." It is imperative for the wealthy man or woman to be vigilant and construct guard rails to protect themselves from infidelity. Here are two guard rails to consider.

The Modesto Manifesto

By 1948, Billy Graham was becoming well known as an evangelist. He was receiving more and more invitations to hold city-wide evangelistic meetings.

Much of the public, however, held a dim view of evangelists because of the misdeeds on the part of some in the past.

During his crusades in Modesto, California, Graham met with his leadership team to discuss the most common criticisms and how they could be above reproach. The Modesto Manifesto was the name they gave among themselves to the principles they decided to apply from that point on.

They committed to exercise extreme care to avoid even the appearance of any sexual impropriety by never being alone with any woman other than their wife or family member. Graham even refused to allow a nurse to come into his hospital room alone while in his 90s! I made the same commitment to Bev decades ago.

Yes, it's been inconvenient at times.

Yes, it's been uncomfortable explaining the reason for this commitment.

Yes, it's been effective.

Covenant with your eyes

When Job was defending his integrity, he said, *"I have made a covenant with my eyes not to look lustfully at a young woman"* (Job 31:1, NIV). This is a standard every man needs to adopt because:

What we gaze upon becomes what we think about.

What we think about becomes what we act upon.

An enormously successful businessman shared with me that in less than a week after making this covenant with his eyes, he and his wife attended a social event. As they were driving home, his wife said, "I don't know what's happened to you, but I'm so much more secure in our marriage since you stopped staring at other women." He had no clue that she had noticed this pattern in life.

The guard rails of never being alone with a woman other than your wife and family members and making a covenant with your eyes will go a long way in protecting you from marital infidelity and help you build an even closer relationship with your spouse.

✏ PERSONAL REFLECTIONS

View the *Radically Improve Your Marriage* video (8:39) by Howard Dayton, or by using this QR code.

- Husbands, what will you do to better fulfill your marital role of loving your wife?

- Wives, how will you better fulfill your marital role of respecting your husband?

22

CHALLENGE OF NOT EXERCISING SPIRITUAL PRACTICES AND FINISHING WELL

I magine that you are a world-class sprinter who has the opportunity to compete in the Olympics representing your country. What will you do to prepare?

You will embark on a rigorous running and exercise program, eat a healthy diet, get adequate sleep, and be trained by an outstanding coach. All this is designed to help you finish the race well.

Just as in athletics, there is practice involved in Christian growth. To go to your favorite place for prayer, for example, is like going to a gym to work out. The extent to which a person grows depends upon these practices. The apostle Paul instructed the younger Timothy to *"Discipline yourself for the purpose of godliness"* (1 Timothy 4:7).

The key practices for finishing well are Bible reading, prayer, serving others, fellowship with other followers of Christ, reading or listening to quality Christian books, worshiping at a vibrant church, and having a very close friendship with at least one or two other believers with whom you have built a deep relationship based on trust, confidentiality, and accountability.

A close walk with Christ is the goal of these practices, and when we remember this, they become a delight instead of drudgery. It's crucial to keep the big picture in mind: the reason to practice spiritual disciplines is not to check another item off our "to do" list; it's to grow closer to Christ. Don't allow this to become a stale exercise; that leads only to frustration.

Bible Reading

No spiritual practice is more important than spending time in God's Word. There is simply no healthy Christian life apart from it. In the Bible, God tells us about Himself. We can learn the ways and will of the Lord. Only in the Scriptures do we find how to live in a way that pleases God and is, as a by-product, the most fulfilling for us.

When Jesus asked people about their understanding of the Scriptures, he often began with the words, "Have you not read?" He assumed that those claiming to be the people of God would have read the Word of God. Unfortunately, this is often not the case. A survey found that only 18 percent of followers Christ read the Bible every day, and 23 percent never do.

When Jesus said, *"Man shall not live on bread alone, but on every word that proceeds out of the mouth of God"* (Matthew 4:4), surely, He intended for us to read every word. Too often, we tend to read Old Testament accounts merely as biblical history without relating them to our lives. However, Romans 15:4 says, *"For everything that was written in the past was written to teach us, so that through endurance and the **encouragement of the Scriptures** we might have hope"* (emphasis added). These principles, commands and stories are meant to inspire us and teach us truth that we can apply to our circumstances.

The Bible makes these remarkable claims about itself: *"The word of God is living and active and sharper than any two-edged sword . . . and able to judge the thoughts and intentions of the heart"* (Hebrews 4:12). *"All Scripture is*

God-breathed and is useful for teaching, rebuking, correcting and training in righteousness, so that the man [and woman] *of God may be thoroughly equipped for every good work"* (2 Timothy 3:16-17, NIV). Since the Bible is living and God-breathed, shouldn't we read and study it?

Here are suggestions for consistent success in Bible reading.

Find the time. Perhaps one of the main reasons Christians never read through the entire Bible is its sheer length. Do you realize that tape-recorded readings of the Bible have proved that you can read through the entire Bible in seventy-two hours? In no more than fifteen minutes a day you can read through the Bible in a year's time. Try to make it the same time every day.

Find a Bible-reading plan. It's no wonder that those who simply open the Bible at random each day soon drop the practice. There are effective Bible-reading plans available, and some Bibles are designed to read through in a year. One of the best is *The Daily Walk Bible.*

Find one phrase or verse to meditate on each time you read. Take a few moments to think deeply about it. This will change your life. The Lord commanded Joshua, *"This book of the law shall not depart from your mouth, but you shall meditate on it day and night, so that you may be careful to do according to all that is written in it; for then . . . you will have success"* (Joshua 1:8). You may be thinking, "That's great for Joshua, but I've got a business or a household to run! I can't think about the Bible all day long. I've got decisions to make. It just isn't practical."

Let me assure you that meditation is the most practical thing in the world. Joshua didn't just sit around all day thinking about the Scriptures. He had two million people to manage. Joshua was as busy, if not busier, than you are. So how does a busy person meditate on the Bible? Read through a portion of the Bible, and when a verse is especially meaningful to you, write it down. Take it with you, review it, and think about it during the day.

Find a Bible study. Most of us will be more consistent if we become involved in a Bible study with others. We need the encouragement and accountability of a group. And one of the greatest benefits is the development of close relationships with others who are seeking to know the Lord better.

Prayer

If prayer could have been unnecessary for anyone, surely it would have been Jesus Christ, the sinless Son of God. However, it was one of the dominant habits of His life and a frequent theme in His teaching.

- He often prayed. *". . . Jesus often withdrew to lonely places and prayed"* (Luke 5:16, NIV).

- He prayed preceding the crucial times in His life and ministry. *"Jesus went out to a mountainside to pray, and spent the night praying to God. When morning came, he called his disciples to him and chose twelve of them, whom he also designated as apostles"* (Luke 6:12-13, NIV).

Even in the midst of His busy public ministry, the Lord consistently spent time alone with His Heavenly Father. Jesus is our supreme example for prayer.

Throughout the history of the church, those serving in leadership have recognized the importance of prayer. Samuel Chadwick said, "The one concern of the devil is to keep Christians from praying. He fears nothing from our prayerless work, prayerless religion. He laughs at our toil, he mocks our wisdom, but he trembles when we pray." And it was John Wesley's conviction that "God does nothing but in answer to prayer."

One of the most important prerequisites to true intimacy with the Lord is honesty in our prayer lives. As C. S. Lewis said, we should "lay before Him what is in us, not what ought to be in us." The Father is pleased that you are willing to come to Him as His child and spend time with Him, so come as naturally as you can. If you are hurting, say so. If you are confused, seek His guidance. If your joy is bubbling over, let it bubble over in praise.

As with reading the Bible, most of us will be more consistent if we establish a regular time in our daily schedule to pray. It is also helpful to establish a list of people and circumstances for which to pray. I have a prayer list that takes about fifteen minutes to pray through. It includes members of my family, close friends, the needs of the Compass staff, and other important situations.

The one concern of the devil is to keep Christians from praying. He fears nothing from our prayerless work, prayerless religion. He laughs at our toil, he mocks our wisdom, but he trembles when we pray." – Samuel Chadwick

Serving

An attitude of service and humility should characterize all we do. Unfortunately, this is contrary to the way many affluent people act toward others.

Jesus told us to be radically different: *"Those who are recognized as rulers of the Gentiles lord it over them; and their great men exercise authority over them. But it is not this way among you, but whoever wishes to become great among you shall be your servant; and whoever wishes to be first among you shall be slave of all"* (Mark 10:42-44).

Only once did Jesus say He was leaving His disciples an example – when He washed their feet to illustrate servanthood (John 13:3-17). It's important to note that the person chosen to lead the children of Israel out of Egyptian captivity was referred to as "Moses, My servant," not "Moses, My leader."

Many who are affluent expect a certain amount of deference. They tend to isolate themselves in comfortable settings surrounded by peers who expect to be pampered. Since wealth is usually served, it is particularly important for those who have been entrusted with resources to seek to serve others.

The Lord can mold us into the people He wants us to become *only as we serve others*, and He often uses our service to benefit us in ways we could not possibly predict.

Fellowship

The Christian life is not one of independence from other followers of Christ but of interdependence with them. Nowhere is this illustrated more clearly than in Paul's discussion concerning the body of Christ in 1 Corinthians 12. Each of us is pictured as a different member of this body. Our ability to function well is dependent on all members working together.

Solomon describes the benefits of dependence on one another: *"Two are better than one because they have a good return for their labor. For if either of them falls, the one will lift up his companion. But woe to the one who falls when there is not another to lift him up. . . . And if one can overpower him who is alone, two can resist him. A cord of three strands is not quickly torn apart"* (Ecclesiastes 4:9-12).

I believe that most of us will *not* finish well without the encouragement and accountability of someone else. It is essential to nurture a relationship with a small group or at least one or two people with whom you have built a friendship based on trust, confidentiality, and accountability. In other words, friends who are close enough and love you enough to confront you if need be. I am more receptive to constructive criticism when it comes from someone I respect and who I know cares for me. *"Iron sharpens iron, so one man sharpens another"* (Proverb 27:17).

For the past three decades, I have benefited immensely from such a relationship with Tim Manor and Jess Correll. We communicate with each other regularly. Other than my wife, they have been my closest friends. One of the most important aspects of our relationships is that we serve one another by holding each other accountable.

Here are several suggestions that will help you identify a small group or friend with whom you can become accountable.

- Pray for the Lord to bring just the right person or people into your life.
- Limit your search to those who you sense are sincere about growing closer to Christ.
- Seek those whose company you genuinely enjoy.

- Do not choose people that you will not be able to trust with confidentiality.

It is also important to be part of a church family. Hebrews 10:24-25 reads, *"Let us consider how to stimulate one another to love and good deeds, not forsaking our own assembling together, as is the habit of some, but encouraging one another; and all the more as you see the day drawing near."*

Reading Christian Books

The person who desires to grow spiritually should read consistently. The doctor who wants to serve his patients well must read to keep abreast of important medical progress. Unfortunately, the habit of reading quality Christian literature is rare.

Because there are so many books available today, it is important to be selective in what you read. We can afford to read only the best – the ones that will be the most helpful to us.

How to read

Reading should involve not only scanning the words but also meditating on the thoughts they express. Charles H. Spurgeon counseled his students: "Master the books you have. Read them thoroughly. Read and reread them. Let them go into your very self. Peruse a good book several times and make notes and analyses of it. A student will find that his mental constitution is more affected by one book thoroughly mastered than by twenty books merely skimmed."

In reading, let your motto be "much, not many." Bacon's famous rule for reading was: "Read not to contradict or confute, nor to believe and take for granted, nor to find talk and discourse, but to weigh and consider. Some books are to be tasted, others to be swallowed, and some few to be chewed and digested."

What to read

The power for good of even one book is impossible to estimate. Reading good biographies should be a major part of a Christian's education. They reveal the importance of godly character, provide illustrations for developing life goals, and teach that sacrifice and self-denial are necessary to fulfill God's purposes. As we read about the lives of men and women powerfully used by the Lord, we become more inspired to invest our lives in building God's kingdom.

Unconditional Surrender

On September 4, 1945, World War II in the Pacific officially ended when Japan unconditionally surrendered to General Douglas MacArthur and the Allies on the U.S.S. Missouri. In war, unconditional surrender involves the conquered submitting fully to the will of the victorious. The defeated usually have no choice.

We who know Christ are called to surrender our will unconditionally to the Lord. God, however, has given us the freedom to choose whether to do it. Unlike the defeated in war, our decision to surrender is motivated by the Lord's unconditional love for us. It is an act of worship. *"Therefore, I urge you, brothers, in view of God's mercy, to offer your bodies as living sacrifices, holy and pleasing to God – this is your spiritual act of worship"* (Romans 12:1, NIV).

Christian leaders have long recognized the importance of this total surrender. Dwight L. Moody said, "The world has yet to see what can happen through a person fully committed to doing God's will." Dawson Trotman, founder of the Navigators, added, "God can do more through one person who is 100 percent committed to Him, than through 99 who are only partially committed."

As we learned earlier in this book, submitting to the Holy Spirit and inviting Him to live His life through us is the only way we will be able to experience Galatians 5:22. *"But the fruit of the spirit is love, joy, peace, patience, kindness, good ness, faithfulness, gentleness, self-control; against such things there is no law."* And as Jesus Christ revealed to us in John 15:5, *"I am the vine, you are the branches; he who abides in Me and I in him, he bears much fruit, for **apart from Me you can do nothing**,"* (emphasis added).

God can do more through one person who is 100 percent committed to Him, than 99 who are only partially committed." – Dawson Trotman, Founder of the Navigators

A Personal Experience

At the risk of being misunderstood by some, I want to share an experience that has fueled my passion to help people learn and apply God's way of handling money. The year was 1977, and I was at home alone when suddenly I was overcome by the Spirit of God and found myself prostrate on the floor, weeping.

While on the floor, the Lord unmistakably and powerfully revealed to me that during my lifetime our nation would experience economic upheaval and a very, very difficult time. God didn't show me when this will occur or what it will be like, but there is no doubt that it will happen.

The financial crises of 2008-2009 and the Covid pandemic that engulfed much of the globe made it clear that the economies of the world are more fragile than most people imagine. So, what should you do to survive and even thrive in the coming economic storm?

Simply be diligent in your efforts to apply what you've learned from the Bible about handling the resources the Lord has entrusted to you. In short, become a faithful steward. One of the best ways to demonstrate your love for your family and friends is to encourage them to do the same.

The *Charting Your Legacy* small group study

I have facilitated more than twenty *Charting Your Legacy* small group studies because I love to see lives change – and *I need it!* About half of the groups have been in person and half virtually over the Internet.

The study is designed for individuals or couples entrusted with much to learn how to finish their lives well. Each group meets for an orientation and six lessons.

Some of the biggest benefits of the *Charting Your Legacy* small group study:

- Close relationships formed among the participants.

- The joy of helping others experience significant life changes

- God's word plows deeper and more indelibly in my heart.

- Those in the group challenge my thinking and encourage me to finish well.

We encourage you to consider what would happen among your friends and peers who have been entrusted with much if they participated in a *Charting Your Legacy* small group study. What would be the spiritual impact in their lives? What would be the influence in their families? What would be the financial effect on the work of Christ in your community and around the world?

Please pray about convening this study to reach others entrusted with much. Visit ChartingYourLegacy.org to explore this in more detail.

Summary

Many people believe that following Christ will be a boring experience – with long faces and endless lists of things you cannot do. Nothing could be further from the truth. The Lord is dynamic, and He intends for us to live vibrant, fulfilling lives. Jesus said it this way in John 10:10, *"**I came that they may have life, and have it abundantly**"* (John 10:10).

Remember an earlier verse. *"Instruct those who are rich in this present world not to be conceited or to fix their hope on the uncertainty of riches, but on God, who richly supplies us with all things to enjoy. Instruct them to do good, to be rich in good works, to be generous and ready to share, storing up for themselves the treasure of a good foundation for the future, **so that they may take hold of that which is life indeed**"* (1 Timothy 6:17-19, emphasis added). Nothing on this planet comes close to knowing Christ and living a life that pleases Him.

Our prayer is that you would finish well and complete the task the Lord has given you so that you will hear these words from the Lord ringing in your ears throughout eternity, *"Well done, good and faithful servant . . . enter into the joy of your master"* (Matthew 25:21).

In addition to these words, meditate on this promise from Christ, *"To him who overcomes* [finishes well] *I will give the right to sit with Me on my throne"* (Revelation 3:21). There is simply nothing more important that finishing well in our journey with the Lord while we are on the earth.

We appreciate the effort you have invested in reading this book. And we pray it has given you a greater appreciation for the Bible, and above all else, nurtured your love for Jesus Christ. May the Lord bless you in every possible way.

My Personal Reflection

As I was finishing the manuscript for *Charting Your Legacy* and after a courageous five-year journey fighting breast and bone cancer, my wife of forty-six years, Bev, went Home to be with the Lord she loved so deeply.

She prayed relentlessly that the Lord would use this book and the *Charting Your Legacy* small group study in the life of every person reading these materials. Our family dedicates *Charting Your Legacy* to a choice servant of God, Beverly Dayton.

🖊 PERSONAL REFLECTIONS

- What can you do to contribute most significantly to the cause of Christ?

- When your life is over, what would you like to be remembered for?

- In light of these answers, what actions or changes to you need to make?

END NOTES

[1] Joe Musser, *The Cereal Tycoon: Henry Parsons Crowell Founder of the Quaker Oats Company*. Moody Publishers, Chicago IL, 1997

[2] John Cortines and Gregory Baumer, *God and Money: How We Discovered True Riches at Harvard Business School*. Rose Publishing, Carson CA, 2016

[3] Jeff Manion, *Satisfied: Discovering Contentment*. Zondervan, Grand Rapids, MI, 2013.

[4] Jerry Bridges, *Trusting God*. Colorado Springs, NAVPRESS, 1988, 2008.

[5] Randy Alcorn, *Money, Possessions, and Eternity*. (Wheaton, IL: Tyndale Publishers, 1989, 2003.)

[6] Steve Farrar, *Finishing Strong*. Colorado Springs: Multnomah Books, 2000.

[7] Claire Cloninger, *Dear Abba*. Nashville: Thomas Nelson, 1997.

[8] David Wills, Terry Parker and Greg Sperry, *Five Questions Every Family Should Ask about Wealth*. National Christian Foundation.

[9] Morgan McCall, *Center for Creative Leadership*.

[10] Johnson, Nichole. "The Dark Side of Halftime." *The Life@Work Journal*. Volume 2. Number 6: 36.

[11] Dr. Haddon Robinson, *Second Chance*.

[12] J. Oswald Sanders, *Spiritual Leadership*. Moody Publishers, Chicago, IL 60610. Several concepts in this chapter and some content are from this outstanding book.

The Compass – *finances God's way*™
Vision, Mission & Values

Our Vision

To see everyone, everywhere faithfully living by God's financial principles in every area of their lives.

Our Mission

Equipping people worldwide to faithfully apply God's financial principles so they may know Christ more intimately, be free to serve Him and help fund the Great Commission.

Core Values

Bible-Based

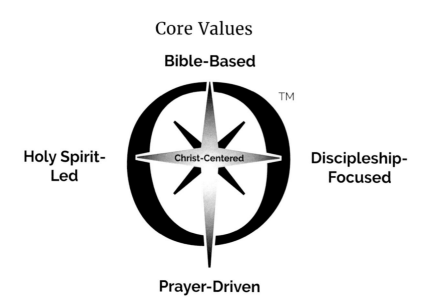

Holy Spirit-Led

Christ-Centered

Discipleship-Focused

Prayer-Driven

Continue The Journey...

Congratulations on completing *Charting Your Legacy.* We hope the Lord has had a significant impact on your financial discipleship journey through this book.

The financial discipleship journey is one that doesn't end until we hear the words *"well done, good and faithful servant."* We encourage you to continue on this journey in one of two ways.

Continue your journey by engaging in studies, tools, and resources that will help you grow. Visit us at **ContinueGrowing.org** to learn more.

Continue your journey by paying it forward and helping others grow. To learn more, visit us at **HelpOthersGrow.org**.

Thank you for the time and effort you have invested in this book. We pray the Lord will draw you ever nearer to Him as you continue to grow and help others grow.

About the Author

HOWARD DAYTON is the founder of Compass–*finances God's way* and cofounder of Crown Financial Ministries. Serving as an unpaid fulltime volunteer at both organizations, Howard also hosted the nationally syndicated radio program MoneyWise. His books and small group studies have been translated into dozens of languages and are used by millions of individuals.

A former naval officer and graduate of Cornell University, Howard's business career was developing office buildings in the Orlando, Florida area. His life radically changed in 1971 when Jesus Christ became his savior. Searching for financial wisdom, he and his partner discovered 2,350 verses in the Bible dealing with money and possessions.

Howard's passion to share the Bible's life-changing principles led him to write eight books and seven small group studies, including Your Money Counts, Money and Marriage God's Way, Business God's Way and Charting Your Legacy. He collaborated with the American Bible Society in the production of The Financial Stewardship Bible.

Howard holds an honorary doctorate from Asbury University. Asbury's Howard Dayton School of Business was renamed the Howard and Beverly Dayton School of Business to honor his wife of 46 years after she died from cancer.

In 2019, Howard married Lynn. Residing in Orlando, Florida, their family includes five adult children and nine wonderful grandchildren.

Compass – *Finances God's Way*™
compass1.org · 407-331-6000